Right Where They Want You

Why You're Not Rich and What to Do about It

"You can't depend on your eyes when your imagination is out of focus."
— Mark Twain

ISBN: 978-0-578-57139-3

Right Where They Want You: Why You're Not Rich and What to Do about It

Copyright © 2019 Kenneth G. Gulliver. All rights reserved. No portion of this book may be reproduced mechanically, electronically, or by any other means, including photocopying, without written permission of the publisher. It is illegal to copy this book, post it to a website, or distribute it by any other means without permission from the publisher.

Ken Gulliver
624 Holly Springs Rd., Suite 207
Holly Springs, NC 27540
Email: ken@ugrucoaching.com
Phone: 800.894.3064

Limits of liability and disclaimer: The author and publisher shall not be liable for your misuse of this material. The author and publisher have taken great care to give credit to the originality of a statement, quote, phrase, etc. In the instance where there may be a miscredit, please notify the author so proper steps may be taken. This book is strictly for informational, educational, and entertainment purposes. The author and publisher do not guarantee that anyone following the ideas, techniques, suggestions, tips, or strategies will become successful. The author and publisher shall have neither liability nor the responsibility to anyone with respect to any loss or damage caused, or alleged to be caused, directly or indirectly by the information contained in this book.

Mark Twain said, "It's easier to fool people than to convince them that they've been fooled." *Right Where They Want You* makes the case that you've been fooled with money, and it shows you what to do about it.

There's a reason they don't teach money in school and, why more people are financially worse each year. Until now, you've only been sold the dream. It's time. Empowerment to fulfill that dream lies in the pages of this book where you'll discover:

- The importance of knowing why you want money.
- How financial advisors make you poor and what to do about it.
- Internal culprits sabotaging success & how to keep them in check.
- Why budgeting doesn't work and how to fix it.
- Why your past hasn't defined you but, prepared you for a great future.
- Why the financial plan your professional completed for you is likely all wrong and what to do about it.
- Tools to synthesize overwhelming and contradictory financial advice, plus so much more.

DEDICATION	VIII
PREFACE	X

1

TRADITIONAL FINANCIAL SERVICES ARE BROKEN 1

"I Get No Respect"	2
Why All the Mistrust?	3
Wait! Where Are You Going?	9
Where Are Advisors *Really* Adding Value?	10
Advisors, What Are Your General Orders?	13
The Consequences of Losing Trust	15
Expectations Not Met	19

2

WERE WE SET UP FOR FAILURE? 21

Flawed Rational Perspective	22
Relying on Past Programming	25
Perspective Is Not Truth	27

3

WHY SOUND FINANCES MATTER 33

Where Sound Finances Start	36
Money: The Great Magnifying Glass	37
Our Past Doesn't Define Us; It Prepares Us.	40

| Learn to take stock | 42 |

4 — ENGINEERED FOR PERFORMANCE ... 45

The Good Book Says…	46
Whatta Ya Know. It Drives Like the Engineer Intended	47
Youthful Ambition, Reckless Pride	49
We Are Only Stewards	51

5 — HOW MUCH LAND DOES A MAN NEED? ... 53

How Much Land Does a Man Need?	54
The Monkey Story	56
And Man Became Ape	57

6 — REAL HEROES KNOW "WHY" ... 59

| 2012: The End of the World (As We Knew It) | 60 |
| 1975: Another Somebody Done Somebody Wrong | 61 |

7 — "IF" AND "WHEN" WERE PLANTED, AND NOTHING GREW ... 65

Your Survival Instinct at Work	66
Hunter and Chase	68
Lights, Camera, Action!	71

8 73

THE BIG LIE WE BUY 73

Have We Put the Cart before the Horse? 74

Three Circles and Three Squares 75

Redemption: Going "Pro" 78

You're at the Bottom of the Food Chain 79

A Value(less) Proposition 81

A Value(less) Proposition – Celebrities 82

A Value(less) Proposition – Financial Advisors 89

A Value(less) Proposition – Insurance Agents 91

The Battle Pushing Investors Away 93

The Case for Financial Coaching 100

A Value(less) Proposition – Google, YouTube, etc. 107

Synthesis: Your Key to Thrive 109

9 111

YOUR FINANCIAL PLAN IS LIKELY WRONG 111

What Financial Planning Is Not 112

What Holistic Financial Planning Is 114

Why Holistic Financial Planning matters 115

Where planning counts most 118

Problems with today's planning philosophy 120

- *Lack of Category-Iterative Planning* 120
- *Long Term Isn't Long Enough* 123
- PROBLEMS WITH TODAY'S PLANNING SOFTWARE 127
- WHY ADVISORS DON'T PROVIDE QUALITY PLANS 142

10 147

LEARN TO THINK FOR YOURSELF 147

- LEARN TO THINK FOR YOURSELF 148
- LET'S MAKE MATH FUN AGAIN! 149
- YOUR RETIREMENT DESTINATIONS 153

11 167

ENSURING YOUR SUCCESS 167

- TUNE IN TO TAP IN 168
- THIS IS THE ULTIMATE "PAY IT FORWARD" IN LIFE 169
- BECOMING A "MEANINGFUL PURPOSE" 172
- FLAWED RATIONAL PERSPECTIVE: REVISITED 178
- CLOSING 179

FINAL THOUGHTS 181

ABOUT THE AUTHOR 183

- KENNETH G. GULLIVER 183

Dedication

To my wife, Cindy, whose understanding and encouragement has strengthened me throughout the years, and my loving children, Leigha and Dax. You may not know it, but I'm fighting for your future, kiddos. To my mother, with whom I have enjoyed so many belly laughs, my Uncle Tom, who inspires me to be a better man (this is me paying it forward), my dad, who gave what he didn't have in support of me, and to my stepmom, who has earned the title "Mom."

To Bob Murphy, who patiently encouraged me to become a financial advisor, and his unforgettable "Honest Immigrant" story. And to all my clients, friends, and enemies, who have all had a hand in shaping me as a husband, father, and businessman, I am eternally grateful.

To all the heroes of faith, who understand how powerful words can be, who believe in amazing possibilities even though they are not seen, and who see their discipline as being so important that they maintain course even in times of weakness.

And finally, to all those who, after great success, will acknowledge the main attribute of success as simple obedience. Receive grace, keep the faith, and fall forward, because the world is watching.

Preface

Thank you for taking the time to read this book. I retired after 20 years as an investment advisor, and there is one astonishing fact that I just can't shake from my head. You see, when I started, 67% of all Americans were unprepared for retirement. Today that number is between 80 and 90%. The point is: traditional financial services are broken; they were from the start.

This book is about you, your relationship with money, and how you can overcome what you may have thought impossible. It's a short journey intended to shed light on the negative view we tend to have about money, the people who are inadvertently (in some cases on purpose) misguiding you, and what to do about it so you can find money you didn't think you had, save money you didn't think you could, and finally have *real* and lasting positive financial change.

The Honest Immigrant
A poor and tattered immigrant walked into a public bathroom upon arriving in the USA. As he entered, he

couldn't help but admire the successful-looking man politely holding the door open for him.

Walking into the stall, he noticed a wallet lying on the floor, bursting at the seams with money. Finding the identification card, he recognized its owner was the same gentleman he had passed while walking into the bathroom.

The immigrant searched high and low and eventually found the owner. The owner was so pleased that such an honest person had found his wallet that he rewarded the immigrant with all the cash the billfold contained.

Years later, the immigrant was interviewed by a local reporter who was interested in the story of how such a poor person could have possibly built the business empire he had.

At the end of the interview, the reporter asked, "Is there anyone you would like to thank for your success?"

The immigrant replied, "I would like to thank the gentleman who held the door open for me."

I hope that this book captivates your imagination and fuels your desire for positive financial change.

Happy reading!

1

TRADITIONAL FINANCIAL SERVICES ARE BROKEN

"My psychiatrist told me I'm crazy. I told him, if you don't mind, I'd like a second opinion. He said, 'Alright, you're ugly too!'"

– Rodney Dangerfield

"I Get No Respect"

The *Forbes* article "Financial Advisers Get Little Respect" quotes a Blackrock Investment survey.[1] The survey took the pulse of investors to better understand their investment behaviors, and it included four thousand investors. The survey uncovered a strong concern about the lack of confidence among U.S. investors. Half do not feel in control of their financial futures and aren't confident they are making the right financial decisions.

Now, you would think they would embrace financial advisors to assist them with these concerns, but that's not what the survey suggested. U.S. retirees in the survey were asked a series of questions about what advice they would give to themselves at a younger age about saving and investing.

Their top three answers:

1. Start saving earlier (36%).
2. Spend less money while working (32%).

---

[1] November 14, 2013.

3. Keep working beyond normal retirement age (21%).

All of these are good ideas (point three depends) that are frequently discussed by financial advisors. But here's the kicker: in retrospect, only 12% of the retirees surveyed said they would have sought professional financial advice.

Isn't that odd? All the advice the retirees would have given themselves would likely have been discussed years earlier had they sought the help of a professional advisor while they were working in their youth. Yet the fact that they wouldn't have sought professional help baffled me. It appeared there was a grave lack of trust for financial advisors. This was a challenge that started bothering me about five years into my advisory career, and I have searched for the answers in my own practice, and for my own success, ever since.

Why All the Mistrust?

There are several reasons I believe people generally don't trust advisors. Some of the biggest culprits are:

Reputation. Advisors have earned a reputation, and it's not a good one. The insurance and equities camps fight against each other, confusing the investor, guys like Bernie Madoff literally steal investor dollars, and shows like *American Greed* showcase these sins and are constantly looking for new material. All of this is on public display, and it's something an advisor who gets up every morning (some of whom are trying to do good for the people they work with) has to constantly fight. Regardless of their intention, this daily fight leads many to unwitting behavior.

Pretentiousness. There is a sense that education, time in the business, and the certificates that hang on a wall will somehow redeem the bad reputation by setting the advisor apart from the industry itself. As well intentioned as this may be, it often comes across as condescending, and if not, the effort to look or sound smart just overwhelms people, making them feel they need to catch up somehow by turning to the internet or friends before they can speak with the advisor again.

Commodification. What I am saying here is that you are most often likely treated as saleable. In other words, you are simply a transaction in the eyes of the financial services industry. In my experience, clients want to be held by the hand as they are led on the journey through their finances by someone they can trust. And trust isn't earned with intellect, education, years in the business, or references; those are mere door openers. There are some well-meaning advisors out there, but they are too small in number to counteract the majority, and they certainly cannot change the rules of the game, at least, not if they continue playing it.

And there's a more far-reaching challenge in play: you have been neatly packaged in a box for future transactions. If an advisor has been in business long enough, someone up the line is going to take issue with what they recommend for you, their client.

There are numerous examples, but the easiest seems to be the neat little box called the "client profile" that advisors are encouraged to perform (I'll outline and discuss the challenges with this later). Maybe you have gone through this exercise with an advisor. For now, let's see it from the advisor's perspective.

For example, let's say that your advisor knows you to be generally conservative, as your answers to the profile questions suggest. Yet a large chunk of assets has already been allocated into highly conservative investments. As your advisor has become familiar with you, you both agree that you should have a portion in an aggressive account. The compliance process they must jump through sets them up, at best, for browbeating and, more likely, rejection. They must conform for the protection of the industry, which has one thing on its mind: moving product.

Product Pushing. Most of us might understand the process better by equating it with the experience we have with our doctors. When we go to the doctor, we expect a consultative approach, yet we are run through the mill with the typical questions:

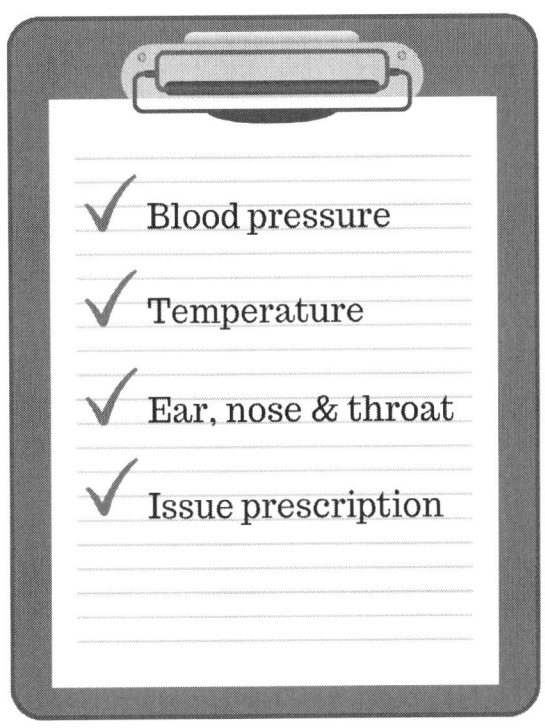

Magic show complete. What if there were something that we could do that was preventative, a lifestyle change that needed to be worked through and monitored? The education of doctors is driven by big pharma, and therefore, drugs are seemingly always the answer.

Financial services and many financial advisors are no different. Don't get me wrong. Most advisors I know want change; they just don't exactly know how to fight through it without losing the life they have built within the confines of the industry. I attempted this when I left my broker-dealer to go independent ("independent" simply means that you are not beholden to sell a company-specified product to your clients). At the time, I hoped to be free to pay attention to my clients in a way that served their best interests, but I was a fish trying to escape by swimming to the other end of the fishbowl.

The financial services industry is driven by heavily marketed investments that are well designed. It's like an addiction to go from one product or portfolio to the next, thinking that buying that next portfolio, annuity, or life insurance policy is the answer. It reeks of similarity to a doctor's visit. Your financial professional (if you have one) is working in a system that wants to see everyone in boxes, and this makes you, the client, feel the same way about advisors as many feel about doctors. I'll dive into this in a later chapter, but that's why holistic planning is so very important.

You can do for yourself what your advisor does for you, but it's easy to feel overwhelmed by all the smart things they talk about. This is right where they want you. Their value depends on it, their career depends on it, and the industry they work in depends on it. I believe you'll understand this after reading the book, but I would submit that you are paying an advisor for an experience. You are looking for a trusted advisor who will walk you on your own journey to financial independence. The question ultimately is: was it a good experience?

Wait! Where Are You Going?

So, if only 12% of us really trust enough to seek continued advice from the pros, where are the other 88% of us going? Well, I suppose it's obvious to state we are getting fed from Google, YouTube, Dave Ramsey, Suze Orman, etc. We are getting it from our plan providers at work, CPAs, attorneys, realtors, and, most recently, through robo-advisors. Oh yeah, I almost forgot our cousin's wife's ex-husband, who has an uncle that's been out of the business for 20 years. I wish I were being funny about that last one, but according to the 2017 Edelman Trust Barometer, "Financial Services Results," financial professionals are now tied with family and friends for trusted advice.

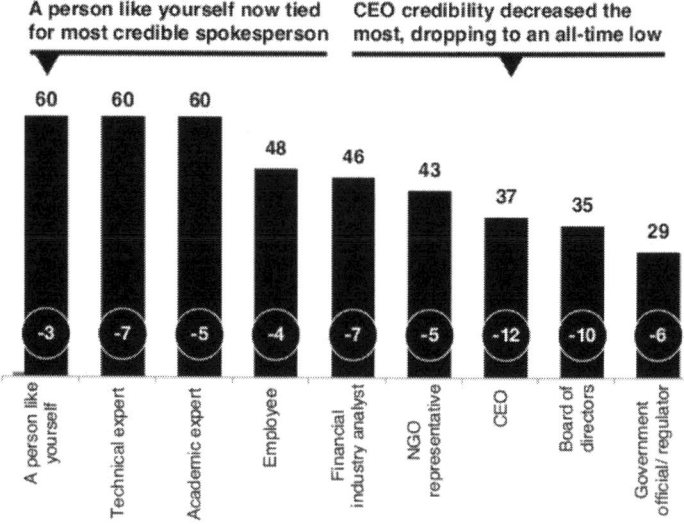

2

"People in this country have had enough of experts."
– Michael Gove, Member of Parliament, U.K.

Where Are Advisors *Really* Adding Value?

That should scare the pros, or at least make them nervous. I'm not an active advisor anymore, and it makes me nervous for them and for you. After all, a person with average intelligence would know the problems with people

---

[2] 2017 Edelman Trust Barometer Q130-747.

searching piecemeal for their financial direction, e.g., through friends, Google, YouTube, etc. But if trust is not re-established (and soon), advisors, as we know them today, could find themselves out of a job completely. My bet? It's over for them already; they just don't know it. That's what happens when you commodify people; they wind up commoditizing you. Now financial services are viewed as the least trustworthy industry, one where lowering their price plays one of the biggest roles in gaining market share. In fact, just yesterday, the news read: "Look Out, Robin Hood. E*Trade, Schwab, Ameritrade go zero-fee."[3] So, where are financial advisors *really* adding value?

---

[3] Techcrunch.com, October 2, 2019.

Financial Services Sector Least Trusted
Percent who trust each industry

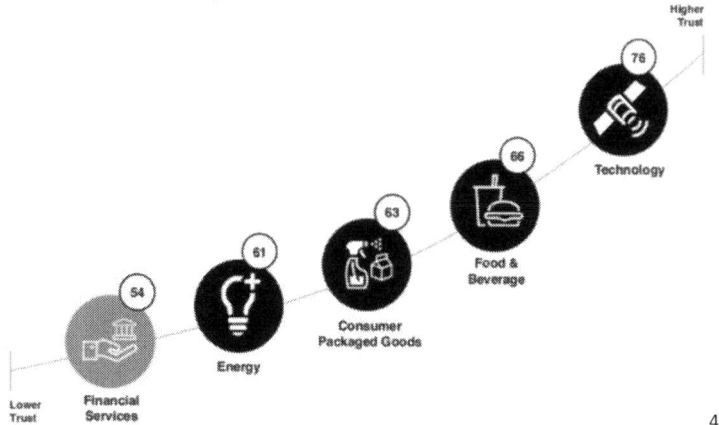

During the industrial age, workers posed one of the biggest challenges to the search for efficiency and profit. They were lazy, wanted smoke breaks, got tired and sick, and sued for more rights. Being smart captains of industry, management found efficiency in systems and machines, eventually adding robots and software. And as the business grew smarter, so did the workers because now they had to manage this technology, and there were fewer positions to fill, meaning increased regulations, more competition, and the need for higher education. Advisors know this as the

---

[4] 2017 Edelman Trust Barometer Q45-429.

SEC, the FINRA, the pursuit of designations, and continuing education (CE). It is no different today for financial services. The investor is the boss, and you will search for a more efficient means to prosperity if you are given reason to.

Advisors, What Are Your General Orders?

"It shouldn't be very difficult for anyone to resist the temptation to force himself into the pattern of the structured man. One needs only to remember that a groove may be safe – but that, as one wears away at it, the groove becomes first a rut and finally a grave."

– J. Paul Getty, *How to Be Rich*

I can hear the words echoing in my head right now: *What are your general orders, recruit!?* When I was in the Marine Corps, we had to memorize our general orders. They were so incessantly seared into our minds that even today I can remember many of them. The purpose of these orders was to ensure safety through vigilance. Without adherence to these orders, we ran the risk of potential havoc.

One of these was our fifth general order, which was: "To quit my post only when properly relieved." This comes to mind because, in my observations, I see a complacent industry. I see an industry quitting its post. I see an industry neglecting the ultimate purpose of its existence (financial services).

Now, I know many who will contradict this idea by suggesting that financial services simply provide the financial tools (mortgages, stocks, bonds, etc.) for someone to achieve their financial goals. And the movement of these tools offered by professionals is a temporary service. Therefore, how can the end-user (you) be neglected? I will acquiesce to that argument if the industry is renamed "financial goods" and the professionals who sell the goods produced change their title from "advisor" to "retailer." Until then, they are derelict in the duty they have defined for themselves, which has consequences.

Financial services, as it has been known, is structured, and that structure is adhered to by professionals (many of whom have the best intentions of helping you). But the very essence of that structure undermines your ability to build true wealth. I say this because, when the emphasis of a "service" industry is placed on moving its product falls short of servicing the end-user, something breaks in the relationship. In the Marine Corps, there could be dire consequences and loss of life if the orders were not carried out, especially if we simply quit our post before our replacement. And if you haven't already, you will soon find there are implications when an industry loses the trust of the public.

The Consequences of Losing Trust

We have seen the trust for the news media plummet recently due to them losing their focus on delivering the facts through great journalism. The media has given up their inheritance of the people's trust for a meal today by taking sides and making sensationalism a priority over true and honest reporting. The consequences of this are a deeper division of our nation's people and petty quarrels that often turn violent or even fatal. Suspicion takes root at every level of life, from friends to government, and becomes a self-perpetuating phenomenon.

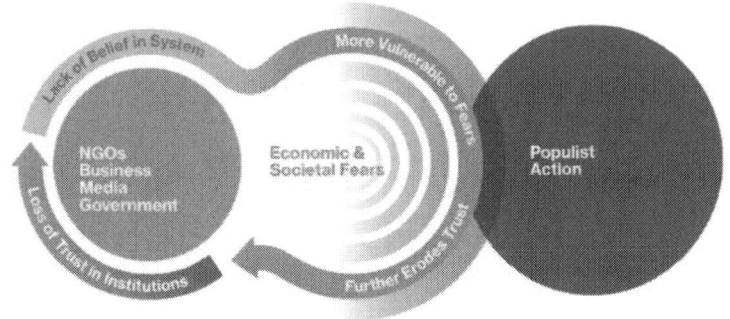

5

What are the consequences of the financial services industry losing our trust, why does this matter, and how far-reaching is this idea? If the very "professionals" who are supposed to be trusted and charged as "gatekeepers" fail to pass working knowledge along in a way that allows for success, then what trajectory does that put us on as individuals, as a community, and as a nation?

I know many advisors who like to focus on the very wealthy. This focus is also encouraged by the companies they work for. One of the firms I worked for forced any client we had with less than $250,000 to an alternative platform with no

---

[5] 2017 Edelman Trust Barometer, Financial Services Results.

personalized service. Needless to say, this deepens the divide between investors and the industry. I know the justification: there isn't enough money for it to be worth the advisors' time. I know this because I heard it regularly and was ridiculed by some of my peers (and management) for spending the same amount of quality time with smaller clients as I did the larger.

The middle and lower classed (and income rich, asset poor) are grossly underserved by financial services, and few have the desire to champion this cause. I believe the only thing standing in the way of that is a change of perspective, which traditional financial services lack. In my opinion, most financial advisors fail to understand:

- The middle and lower classes need direction just as much as the wealthy. Scratch that; they need it more.
- Advisors are ambassadors. It's important to recognize they are representative of stewardship. Forgetting that leads to a widespread negative view from the investing public, making it harder for people to gain hope for prosperity.

- They will make far more money (I did). You cannot enrich yourself unless you enrich others. In other words, when they empower us as opposed to selling us, we become raving fans. And an army of advocates will bring their wealthier friends to the table. Bonus!
- If people aren't educated and cared for, they become adversarial, which manifests itself in movements that elect officials whose constituents insist on higher taxes for the wealthy and free health care, not to mention activism like Occupy Wall Street. All of this breeds an ignorance that erodes what would otherwise be a thriving marketplace for their advice.

If perspective remains unchanged, it begs the questions: Who is going to stand between people and the real enemy of poverty (ignorance)? Who is going to be the man/woman of the "in-between"? Failing to consider the consequences of losing trust has implications for our nation of the highest degree.

Expectations Not Met

I remember what I expected as a new advisor. It started out full of grandeur, but then experience set in. The first company I started working with, in 1996, was beyond exciting to me. I had high hopes for the future but soon understood that we were product salesmen and were dangerous because we really weren't professionals and only understood a sliver of the scope of what we should have been doing. Deep down inside, I wanted to be of *value* to people. It's what I expected that I should be and what I knew was right.

So, I took (among many others) my Series 7 test. I enrolled at the College for Financial Planning to pursue my CFP, and I hired on with a more "professional" company. As I sat in the office on my first day of work, I was relieved to be working with professionals at a respectable firm. After all, I expected *respect*.

I remember talking to all the tenured advisors at this new firm. One conversation on the first day raised my eyebrow. For reasons I will share in a later chapter, I realized we weren't helping people much more. For now, I'll just share that I expected to work with *integrity*.

So, I started my own registered investment advisory firm, and I had plenty of ideas that were new and different. I expected to be *unique*, but I was blocked by regulatory agencies that made it logistically and financially difficult for me to exercise these ideas because it didn't fit in their box. Adding to this, I was bogged down with the day-to-day tasks of managing growth and technology that was supposed to make life easier.

One day I asked myself: What happened to those dreams? When did value get traded for commodification? How was the respect from the general population lost? Where was integrity? How and why had advisors become commoditized? And the most baffling question of all: why did it seem like the masses didn't want help? Why did they complain about their situation but remain so aloof?

2

WERE WE SET UP FOR FAILURE?

"Those who improve with age embrace the power of personal growth and personal achievement and begin to replace youth with wisdom, innocence with understanding, and lack of purpose with self-actualization."

– Bo Bennett.

Flawed Rational Perspective

You've said it a thousand different ways, a thousand different times:

> Wampum, dough, sugar, clams, loot, bills, bones, bread, bucks. Money. That which separates the haves from the have-nots.
>
> But what is money? It's everything if you don't have it, right? Half of all American adults have more credit card debt than savings. About 25% have no savings at all, and only 15% of the population is on track to fund even one year of retirement.
>
> Suggesting what? The middle class is evaporating? Or the American dream is dead? You wouldn't be sitting here listening to me if the latter were true.
>
> You see, I think most people just have a fundamentally flawed view of money. Is it simply an agreed-upon unit of exchange for goods and services? Is it $3.70 for a gallon of milk? Thirty bucks to cut your grass? Or is it an intangible? Security or happiness? Peace of mind?
>
> Let me propose a third option: money as a measuring device. You see, the hard reality is that how much money we accumulate in life is not a function of who's president, the economy, bubbles bursting, or bad breaks or bosses. It's about the American work ethic. The one that made us the greatest country on Earth.

> It's about bucking the media's opinion as to what constitutes a good parent. Deciding to miss the ball game, the play, the concert because you've resolved to work and invest in your family's future – and taking responsibility for the consequences of those actions.
>
> Patience. Frugality. Sacrifice. When you boil it down, what do those three things have in common? Those are choices. Money is not peace of mind. Money is not happiness. Money is, at its essence, the measure of a man's choices.

Money. It is a measuring stick, but in the above monologue from the Netflix TV series *Ozark*, the rationale that money can somehow only be present in abundance by deciding to make it more important than quality life is flawed. The character who delivered this monologue is a man after money for the wrong reasons. I know a little bit about that. You see, I've spent much of my life pursuing money, shifting from one flawed rationale to another.

Nevertheless, money is the measure of a person's choices. It's not simply measured by the amount you have in your account, though. It's also measured by how it has enriched the finer areas of your adult life.

Children don't understand money the way adults perceive it. But children do know the feelings that come with having it or not having it, and those experiences metastasize into behaviors that follow us, often to our grave. I remember my parents arguing about money. I remember more money being spent on cigarettes and beer than on my clothing. I remember kids saying, "Haha, you know its Kenny coming. Just look at his shoes." I remember child support being used to buy unnecessary living room furniture. The list goes on for me, as I'm sure it does for you.

For a child, it's hard to reconcile those moments in their life, let alone articulate what they have experienced. And at the ripe young age of 18, as we stare out at a vast new future filled with unknown terrors and the promise of unfilled dreams, we proceed to live what appears to be an adult life: we have a job, a car, an apartment.

But without "understanding" and "reconciliation" of our experiences, we're set up for failure, because we cannot win a game that we don't understand. Many of us have been programmed for failure, with that small voice of those experiences subconsciously telling us how to make decisions. This voice tells us that cigarettes and beer are more important than clothing or that financing a living room set will make you happy. And if our spouses question our actions or motives, the voice tells us to defend ourselves at all costs.

There is an old passage you may have heard: "Give a man a fish, and he can eat for a day. Teach a man to fish, and he can feed himself for a lifetime." Without going through the process of learning to "fish," that voice continues to play: "Good money spent on cheap things is comfortable and must be right because it's all I've ever known."

Relying on Past Programming

As long as that voice plays in the back of our minds, our actions are on autopilot, making us reliant just as we were when we were kids.

We're the same kids we were on the playground; we've just learned how to hide it better. We act like adults by appearing to have it all together with that job, car, and house. And we're even proud to use credit cards on friends after fine dining.

But the definition of "adult" is far more expansive than those basics. The defining word for being an adult is "responsible" – in other words, being able to respond.

Without gaining the ability to respond, we're still reliant. Reliant on money? Possibly, but if not, reliant on

1. Information found on the first page of a Google search.
2. Fast food to feed us.
3. Medicine to fix an unhealthy lifestyle.
4. A degree over becoming educated.
5. Society to raise our children.
6. Social Security for our retirement.

That voice becomes the shaping force of our future. I want to shape my own future, and I'm sure you feel the same.

When we don't think critically for ourselves, we leave our future to outside forces telling us what to do, how to live, and what level of prosperity we should have.

When too much reliance is placed on outside forces to take care of us, it not only hurts the people who are hardworking and self-reliant, but it also hurts the people receiving the handout.

Perspective Is Not Truth

"If you change the way you look at things, the things you look at change."
– Dr. Wayne Dyer

I believe it is important to understand that the perspective we have about money is likely not our own. The perspective that we have is built from years of listening to a well-intentioned person, TV, radio, or some other form of media that we find credible simply because the masses are plugged into the same programming.

I recently read an article titled "Americans Believe in Science, Just Not Its Findings." Although only two thousand people were surveyed, I found the disconnect between scientists and people to be interesting. In the survey, 80% generally believed science had made life easier, but there was a disparity on many topics. For instance, 88% of scientists said genetically modified foods were "generally safe" to eat, but only 37% of the public agreed. The humor was in climate change, where 94% of scientists said it was a "very serious" or "somewhat serious" problem, while 65% of the public agreed. However, though most of those scientists blamed humans, only 50% of the public agreed with that.

My point is: what we follow tends to be a touchy-feely thing. We like it if it serves us and dislike it if it doesn't. We believe in an objective process, but we are subjective in our behavior. Some might write this off as human nature, like the 80/20 rule. I believe there is a reason the 80% behave the way they do, and I also believe the 80% are not sentenced to remain where they are.

In my observations, very few people go through an objective process to determine whether they buy into a particular ideology. There are many reasons I suppose people choose to follow another's opinion without question. However, having sat with thousands of people on the topic of their personal finances, I have found the main reason they have blindly followed is that they weren't taught how to think for themselves. So, it seemed easier to follow, easier to listen, easier to believe a professional must know more than we do, and easier to sue those professionals (not really) when it all falls apart. Their perspective was not their truth. That's a painful discovery process, but there is another way.

Professionals in financial services are human like you. When I started my career, I followed the assumption that whoever was teaching me knew more than I did and, therefore, it was paramount for me to focus on being a good student. Of course, it's imperative to have a solid foundation of knowledge, so I wanted to be a good student. But later I found areas that did not serve me well and, at the same time, didn't serve my clients.

For example, for many years, I bought into the idea that there was an optimal way to distribute assets when funding a retirement. I bought into this idea because it's taught in financial schools. Ask any CPA, financial advisor, or other financial professional what they subscribe to as the best way for the distribution of your assets, and they will tell you: "Use the lowest-yielding, highest-taxed assets first and then work your way to the next, following suit until your assets are exhausted."

I followed this methodology for years until I had the opportunity to develop my own software. I was tired of trying to complete financial plans for clients with software that fell short of what I needed to do my job.

As I architected my planning software, one of the areas worked on was this idea of asset distribution. When I started, I didn't think much of it other than the calculations needed to be accurate, but I fully expected the outputs to fall in line with what I was taught and what was conventional wisdom in financial services.

What I found left me reeling. I went round and round, making sure the math was right, because I was finding that the standard advice taught for asset distribution was wrong over 60% of the time. The more I double- and triple-checked the math, the more I wished it was incorrect, because that meant I had steered many a client in the wrong direction; it's hard to admit you're wrong, especially when you are supposed to be the professional.

Conventional wisdom is often not so wise. As the definition of "conventional" states, it is "based in accordance with what is generally done or believed," not on fact. Therefore, when we follow conventional wisdom, we are following suit. Some would more succinctly refer to this as being lazy.

Perspective is not truth, but it does become our modus operandi, or the way we operate. If someone wished to control you but make you feel like you were free and that it was your decision, then that is the ultimate way to gain conformity with you, as well as with the masses.

Since the beginning of time, man has wanted to control man. Whether it's a king exercising power to brutalize subjects, the modern-day government seeking a docile constituency, or private business controlling your mind through psychology-based marketing, they change our perspective, so we fall in line with their agenda. And the younger we can be indoctrinated, the easier it is for them to control us.

We *want* to get up, go to work, and take on debt to buy the shiny new car, bigger house, and newest technology and take expensive vacations. Sadly, many of us want it that way even though it leaves us broke. But it robs us of true financial independence in exchange for a false sense of success, and it can only last as long as we can keep running on the hamster wheel.

This is right where they want you. It's also why many of us have a deep longing for financial independence. Somewhere deep inside, we know that it's our ticket out of bondage, but the what, how, and why elude us.

3

WHY SOUND FINANCES MATTER

"Money is the great magnifying glass. It makes a good person better and a bad person worse."

– Anonymous

When people lack the knowledge *of* their finances or lack the engagement *in* their finances, it causes a ripple effect that harms the greater society and, moreover, ourselves, which is why having sound finances is so important. I'll start by sharing six reasons to have sound finances.

1. Malnutrition. People in poverty rarely have access to nutritious foods, leading to the "McDonalds" effect, which brings me to the second point.

2. Health. Diseases are common in people living in poverty because they lack the resources for a healthy living environment. Physically and financially, yes but, also their values like the next point.

3. Education. There's a clear correlation between poverty and lack of education. Not valuing education leads to illiteracy and ignorance.

4. Economy. An illiterate and ignorant workforce hinders a country from developing into a strong economic system.

5. Society. Unemployment opens the doors to homelessness and social unrest, leading to increased crime.

6. Anxiety. Even if you think you've won the battle and conquered poverty, statistically, you're suffering from great anxiety.

According to the National Alliance on Mental Illness (NAMI), almost 44 million Americans live with anxiety disorder. Worse yet, one half begins at the age of 14! Ten million Americans struggle with co-occurring mental health disorders, meaning addictions like alcoholism, gambling, or drugs. And one-fourth of the homeless and prisoner populations is a result of these mental disorders.

Furthermore, the impact is that depression resulting from anxiety is the number one cause of disability worldwide. It's responsible for 90% of suicides. The cost to the United States alone is $200 billion per year.

I feel the reason a cure has not been found is money itself. After all, big pharma is a one-trillion-dollar industry, far larger than the $200 billion cost of the illnesses they treat.

Where Sound Finances Start

Having sound finances starts with making sound financial decisions. You see, success and failure are not big events. They're the aggregate of many small decisions. Many know this, so they promise themselves to make sound financial decisions.

Making a promise is a start, but we're talking about fighting years of hardwiring in our brains, years of evolving into how we live today.

My idea of man's evolution is a little different. I'm not talking Mel Brooks's *History of the World, Part I*: *Twenty million years ago, an ape-like creature inhabited the earth...and the ape stood and became man.*

I see the timeline in a single lifespan. First, the desire for food and shelter is essential. Then we develop into people seeking safety and security. Then relationships become important, often because of safety and security. Then we evolve into reaching our full potential, and somewhere along the line, we find ourselves searching for more.

Unable to pinpoint what that "more" is, we default to the pursuit of more money and more things. More money, more things, more money, more things (zombie voice).

Somewhere along the span of our own lives, we found the hurt and unfulfillment, possibly from a childhood that still tells us we're less important than beer and cigarettes and leaving us with gaping holes in our hearts that we fill with cheap things we pay good money for. It can be hard to see, but it's a vice like any other addiction.

For many people, it may sound simple to escape a vice, but in the addicted person's world, it seems impossible to break, which is evidenced by the staggering costs associated with addiction.

I read an article recently in *US News* that said: "The yearly annual economic impact from the misuse of prescription drugs, illicit drugs or alcohol is half a trillion dollars."

Money: The Great Magnifying Glass

As I have walked this earth and have had the honor to know the many people who have entrusted me with their financial direction, it's become my unwavering belief that *money* is the biggest addiction, eclipsing all others combined.

I also believe that money is the catalyst for other addictions. And when I think about the many books written about money and the many that I have read throughout the years, *Rich Dad Poor Dad*, *The Millionaire Next Door*, etc., the one that stands out for me by far is the Bible.

You see, money is the great magnifying glass. It makes a good person better and a bad person worse, so humankind needed instructions on how to handle it. Money is an incredibly powerful medium when it comes to putting into motion what lies in the heart. Like the old saying goes: "Show me your check register, and I'll show you where your heart is."

If money were not such a powerful tool for both good and evil, if money weren't such a potentially pervasive part of our lives, it wouldn't be mentioned so often in books like the Quran, the Vedas, the Tripitaka, and the Bible, which mentions it over two thousand times.[6] Two thousand three hundred and fifty times, the Bible makes a point of money and possessions, far more than any other topic outside of God Himself. Do sound finances matter? You bet they do.

So, if you have any limiting beliefs about money, no amount of organizing a spreadsheet is going to help you pay off your debt or save for the future in a lasting and fulfilling way. And you'll always wonder how others magically make it.

In the end, you'll dislike yourself and others more, and you'll be disgusted with everything related to money. It will have become evil to you.

And worse, unlike other addictions, it's contagious. Parents will pass on their limiting money beliefs to their children, sentencing them to the same struggles, or they'll compensate so radically that most won't tolerate their presence.

---

[6] https://www.forbes.com/sites/sherylnancenash/2012/05/24/is-the-bible-the-ultimate-financial-guide/#1bfbe6086493.

Our Past Doesn't Define Us; It Prepares Us.

I'm quite sure we've all been adversely affected by money choices in some way, but there's a beauty to having had money problems in our past.

Noteworthy: Our past doesn't define us; it prepares us.

I grew up in a lower-middle-class family, and money was at the center of much of the heartache I felt. No one taught me about money; I had to learn the hard way.

Countless times, I had to remind myself: *I'm not being punished; I'm being prepared*. We should all remember that bad things don't happen to us; they happen for us.

I remember leaving Merrill Lynch in 2006 and starting my investment advisory practice. Life was getting ready to teach me a lesson I would never want to forget.

I had a huge house, my health, the respect of the community, and a small financial practice that employed 20 people. I owned a boat in San Diego, part of a dental practice in Arizona, and a seven-passenger private jet. My home was decorated by a hired professional and adorned with a Steinway baby grand piano. I was smart and in control.

Life seemed perfect in many ways – except one. I'd spent well over a decade with a woman that I simply wasn't meant to be with. We were both wasting time trying to make a wrong decision right, and coming from a broken family, the last thing I wanted was my kids to experience the pain of Mommy and Daddy getting a divorce. I don't condone divorce, but after 17 years, I could no longer cope by filling the gaping holes in my heart with material things.

Life is fragile, and our financial house can be brought down overnight. For me, it was the divorce. It wasn't immediate, though. Nearly two years after the divorce was final, I met the woman of my dreams, and something happened. The floor dropped out from underneath me.

I was served with a legal notice trying to break up the divorce. The process took three years and included a child custody battle. In the middle of this was the real estate and stock market collapse in '08. The house, financed for $650k, dropped in value to $280k. The piano was given up, the boat sold for pennies on the dollar, and the jet given away at a loss of nearly $2 million.

I traveled ten thousand miles per month, and clients required the utmost attention. I was sleep-deprived, a nervous wreck, and I just knew people were only nice to me because of my money. People collectively OWED ME $650k! And I owed twice that in debt.

Mentally, emotionally, and financially spent, I faced bankruptcy. I was humiliated and hurt, and I didn't know who my friends were. I swore that from that moment on, I would count the cost before any purchase and always aspire to be debt-free. I'd never done that before.

Most years, I'd made enough money to cover up my transgressions, so I never bothered with accounting for what I had spent my money on. Because of that, I failed to comprehend the dire situation I was getting myself into. Life had gotten in the way.

Learn to take stock

Don't you love it when life gets in the way? The experience of losing so much from spending good money on cheap things taught me that if you don't measure something, you can't understand it. If you can't understand it, you can't control it. If you can't control it, you can't improve it.

Noteworthy: Learn to take stock.

If we don't learn to take stock, we'll pursue what we want and fail to get what we need to have, its right where they want you. Needs, like peace of mind and financial freedom, are long term and bring us joy. Things we want like a shiny new car or technology is short term and can only bring us short term happiness.

Noteworthy: I promise I won't let short-term wants get in the way of long-term needs.

To do that, you need to take stock by keeping a budget. While people don't stick with their budgets, they're increasingly searching how to budget. In fact, from 2004 to 2019, Google searches for "how to budget" increased threefold, and many of those searches are people returning to find a better mousetrap.

Why don't they stick with their budget, and why are they increasingly looking for something that might work better than the last time they tried? Maybe they think:

1. It's not fun tracking my spending.
2. I don't have enough money to budget.
3. I get too many paper cuts stuffing envelopes.

I believe I know the reason. You see, before you can stick with and master your budget, you need to make giving a part of it.

4

ENGINEERED FOR PERFORMANCE

"The world we live in is a useable world, and if we don't use it in the right way, it can be a cruel world."

– Anonymous

The Good Book Says...

The Good Book says that if we give a tenth of our income, the windows of heaven will open and pour out so many blessings that we won't have enough room to receive them.

Think about that for a second. The windows of heaven will open and pour out blessings! Can you imagine that?

Because it seems so ridiculous, we tend to think it's not practical. And if we don't see the practicality in something, chances are we won't do it.

There is one interesting fact about that passage. To delineate, the Hebrew word "*nacah*" (naw-saw'), which means "to test," is found 36 times in the Bible.[7] Each time, it's used as a warning not to test God or to show that He's proven something to us. But the word "*ubehanuni* (u-ve-cha-nu-ni), which, literally translated, means "and try me,"

---

[7] https://www.bibletools.org//index.cfm/fuseaction/Lexicon.show/ID/H5254/nacah.

is an open invitation to test Him and is found only once in the Bible.[8]

When I grew up, words like that were used to take up the gauntlet, like when Mom said, "Do that again. Juuust try me!"

Whatta Ya Know. It Drives Like the Engineer Intended

I believe we're invited to give because He knows us. Think about it this way: who knows more about your car, you, the local mechanic, the factory mechanic, or the original engineer?

You may have read the owner's manual. The local mechanic may be able to fix the car, and the factory mechanic will fix the car to spec, but the engineer designed the car, calculated every part, tested it in a wind tunnel, on the track, in hot and cold weather, and ran thousands of other

---

[8] https://biblehub.com/text/malachi/3-10.htm.

tests that put it through its paces. Essentially, the engineer knows why your car behaves the way it does.

You see, we came from the factory with this little string. It's connected to our spending hand, and it goes all the way around to our backside. I won't say where it's connected to, but I will tell you this: when our spending hand gives the first of our earnings, that string pulls on something back there and makes it tighter, if you know what I mean. It's one of the many autopilot functions we were built with.

When we operate ourselves the way we were intended, life is easier. I heard someone once say, "The world we live in is a useable world, and if we don't use it in the right way, it can be a cruel world."

You see, without "giving," we work harder for everything because we are missing the element of accountability that is uniquely put in motion when we give.

And working harder for money means more and more focus on the superficial and less focus on the meaningful.

Youthful Ambition, Reckless Pride

I was an ambitious young man. And like many ambitious young men, everything I did or accomplished was another trophy in life. In fact, I have a three-ring binder I kept all my accomplishments in. I used to quip that it was my "I-love-me book."

We didn't have Facebook back then, so I had to scrapbook my ego. And I couldn't get enough. I joined the Marine Corps, bought my first house when I was 22, and had two rentals. I owned a company, was making $12k per month, and, at the young age of 23, became a financial advisor.

I was one of the youngest branch managers, earned a senior executive position with the company, where I recruited hundreds of people, and gave motivational talks, and all of it was scrapbooked.

In my efforts to gain even more, I left that company in pursuit of more money. I was owed an ongoing percentage of all my hard work, so I was confident about the transition, but when I left, about a hundred other people also left for the new company, which was a breach of contract.

Now, because I understood this and didn't want to lose what I was owed, I promptly resigned and wrote a letter to my old company, explaining that my departure wasn't malicious, that I wasn't trying to poach, and that as an act of good faith, I'd resigned from the new company.

The response was interesting. After six and a half years with a spotless record, I received six complaints over a couple weeks. Of course, no company was going to hire me until they were resolved.

Fast forward, and I was finally absolved of any wrongdoing. In fact, I found out that the complaint letters had been contrived by someone above me who had lost a lot of money when I'd left.

Nevertheless, the experience took nine agonizing months of income out of my pocket. I was crushed. I had no idea what had just happened.

You know the feeling you get when something so bad happens to you? Like when someone you love decides to leave you? The pale, tingling, and stunned sensation that crawls all over your skin?

That was me, and I had no answer. I could have worked in another industry, but I didn't. Maybe I was too proud, or maybe I was too scared to lose my identity, but I didn't do anything.

I was so depressed that I spent the last of my money eating, I lost my family because I couldn't provide for them, and I found myself all alone, with no money, no job, and no food.

I had a three-month supply of vitamins, tap water, and half a loaf of molding bread. I was starving to death – literally! I lost 50 pounds in 90 days, and I was so weak. The pain of starving is like no other.

We Are Only Stewards

What I didn't know was that I was learning a solid money principle. Before I learned this principle, it didn't quite matter which idea I had to make more money or find a good opportunity, because, no matter where I went or what I did, there I was. Instead of scrapbooking my ego, I should have scrapped my ego. What do you think?

I learned that nothing we have in the world is ever ours. Not our money, not our possessions, not our bodies. We're only stewards of what we are blessed with.

Until that time, I thought everything I had was mine. Even my success in business. I was right where they wanted me. And because it was a self-serving attitude, my desires were insatiable. Because I lacked a sound reason for wanting money, I didn't know what to do when I had it. I was like a dog chasing a car. Please, what are you really gonna do when you catch it? You cannot break the rules of the universe and expect fulfillment; it's impossible.

5

HOW MUCH LAND DOES A MAN NEED?

"We're the same kids today that we were on the playground. We've just learned how to hide it better."

– Ken Gulliver

How Much Land Does a Man Need?

It's been said that God's address is at the end of your rope. So, it makes sense that while in the depth of my crisis, I found myself watching a televangelist.

This gentleman was telling a story of a man fueled by greed. I'd later find that the story was from Leo Tolstoy: "How Much Land Does a Man Need." This story inspired me to write a poem.

Their once was a hardworking farmer who toiled into the night.

He gripped the hoe and milked the cows, much to his wife's delight.

Yet in his heart, he knew working as a peasant was reserved for a fool...

If I had more land, I'd be my own man. Not even Satan would have a demand.

But the devil was present and rose to the challenge of the pride in his new friend.

So, he sent two demons to work a plan for this arrogant man.

The details of this took just a whisper, you see...

A seed of greed and a seed of fear are all the two parties would hear.

One for the farmer to find a great deal and the other a village in need of his skill.

Yes, this was the place where he'd have crops abundant and never run out.

This land was cheap, and the people were simple. What a great deal no other found out.

Yet with a low price came a small sacrifice, which the village demanded up front.

These simpleminded people asked just one thing; consequence to the farmer was unseen.

At a sunrise start, you must walk the land and mark the ground as you make your way.

But return at sundown, or you'll be let down, as you won't be offered a rock.

With this, he embarked on a warlike march, spading the ground with a smile.

But to his surprise, the glare in his eyes soon sat low in the sky.

So, he hurried his way in great dismay that he might not make it by dusk.

And as he stepped on the last blade of grass, he ended his journey, weakened and beat.

He walked an expanse of land, so much more than he could command, but the story wasn't over, you see.

To all the tribe's glee, the farmer took his last knee and collapsed in front of them, spent.

His servant gave him a grave, while his wife stood bereaved, yet the farmer found his peace.

It's the hardworking man who makes his last stand, which his survivors will ask:

How much land does a man need?

Fortunately, my starvation event didn't kill me. When we go through bad times, it can feel like it. Part of me did die, though. You see, I found myself with a changed heart. I realized that before I could ever build real and lasting wealth, I would first need to learn to give. I know it may sound odd to you, so let me explain this idea another way.

The Monkey Story

In some parts of the world, monkeys can be a problem. They raid and destroy most everything at will and are generally a nuisance, even a danger to the human population. They're quick and agile, so the only way to catch them is to be smarter than the monkey. As it turns out, monkeys have a huge flaw in their personality: if they see something they like, especially food, they just won't let it go.

So, the locals facing this kind of challenge simply place a jar of peanuts out in the open for the monkeys to enjoy. Eventually, curiosity gets the best of one of the monkeys, and it places its hand in the narrow jar opening and grabs a big handful of peanuts. To the monkey's frustration and terror, it can't remove its hand. As much as it tries, it just can't pull that fistful of peanuts out! While the monkey is hampered by the heavy jar, the locals move in and throw a net over it for relocation. It's ridiculous, but it's just not in the nature of a monkey to let go.

And Man Became Ape

Think about it. Monkeys are intelligent, so intelligent they fashion tools to help them get along in this world. Yet they'll trade a few extra peanuts for possibly their life! So, it's not a matter of intelligence that the monkey gets trapped. It's a matter of behavior. Monkeys operate with the idea that if they let go, they'll wind up empty-handed, even though it's plain to see that if they just released their grip on the handful of peanuts, they could have the whole jar.

Humans can be the same way. We buy things we fall in love with: a new car, a house, some technology, or even small purchases we think are harmless until we see the frequency at which we make those purchases. When money gets tight, we tend to grab on tighter to these things, and they become the reason for our financial downfall.

Letting go is a prerequisite of wealth building. Without learning to let go, we fail to grasp our authentic reasons for having money.

Noteworthy: Learn to let go.

6

REAL HEROES KNOW "WHY"

"You do not have because you do not ask. When you ask, you do not receive because you ask with wrong motives."

– James 4:3

2012: The End of the World (As We Knew It)

I remember it was 2012, and my wife and I had been dreaming and talking about our future, as we often do. You know, dreaming is so important. Without dreams, you'll eventually give up on yourself. So, we were dreaming about our next life move.

We were financially free and excited about what the future held. But every time we dreamed, I had a deep tugging in my heart about what was important in life. My family was a priority, and we were going to be empty nesters soon, so our talk was primarily about plans to retire early and live *our* lives the way *we* saw fit.

The political landscape was causing a deeper divide in the United States than I'd ever remembered, and we just wanted to run away from the chaos. But there was that tug again, a small voice in the back of my head: *Ken, what's more important? Your money or me?*

Actually, it sounded more like: *Ken, I am your father. What's more important, money or me?* (Darth Vader voice)

I said this earlier: we're the same kids today that we were on the playground. We've just learned how to hide it better. You see, what God knew about me is that I was getting ready to do the same thing I had done almost 40 years earlier.

1975: Another Somebody Done Somebody Wrong

Let's take a trip back in time to a simpler life, a life where people were kinder, where they cared about each other more. Let's take a trip back to 1975, to when little Kenny was at his babysitter's.

Little Kenny hated this place. To this day, I have scars from being burned on my legs and arms. They used to think it was funny to ask if I wanted to see a match burn twice.

"Hey, Kenny! Want to see a match burn twice?" "Yeah! That would be cool…" Then they would strike it, blow it out, and touch me with it. It was like a sadistic version of 52 pickup and, I remember coming home with ticks on me. It was a horrible place!

As you can imagine, by the time my mother picked me up, I was ready to run away! One time, I saw her walking up to the front door, and I turned to the babysitter and gave them the bird, yelling out, "Rut rooo!" Then I turned and ran out.

Fast forward 40 years, and God knew I was ready to say, "Rut rooo!" to the world. And money? Money was my ticket out. I was trying to run, but the hounds of heaven smelled blood. You see, I'd been here before. God says He disciplines the ones He loves, but I'd been disciplined before and didn't like it.

Don't get me wrong, I wouldn't trade the outcome for a million dollars, I just didn't want it again. How's that old saying go? "Everyone wants to go to heaven, but no one wants to die."

Back to 2012. My wife and I were dreaming about retiring when the tugging at my heart was calling for something different. Of course, because I was a bratty little kid, I did what I wanted, which forced me to spend down my life savings, sell the house, and use the proceeds of my financial practice to ensure *my* decision was right. Talk about making a wrong decision right. Boy, do we get stuck to our money. That experience tested my resolve to work, as well as how I felt about God. In case you're wondering, yep, I had a few choice words for Him.

I learned that money is a two-edged sword and that a whole different set of principles are at play when you have it. I was being prepared, because, without that experience, you wouldn't be reading this book and UGRU wouldn't exist, which opens the possibilities for the masses to learn something that has been actively kept from them their whole lives.

It also became clear that I had a hero complex. It's the reason I had joined the Marine Corps three decades before, but what I later learned was that the word "hero" comes from the Latin word *"servare,"* which means to save or protect, literally meaning to be a servant of others. This really put into perspective my motivation for money.

James 4:3 reads: "You do not have because you do not ask. When you ask, you do not receive because you ask with wrong motives." That's frustrating, isn't it? Money feels like an enigma to most people, but if we change our perspective, we can find joy in what most people perceive as a struggle because the testing of your faith will produce perseverance and that perseverance makes us mature and complete, needing nothing. Needing nothing.

To change your perspective, ask yourself:

1. What financial challenges have you overcome?
2. What was the impact of those challenges?
3. What new possibilities opened as a result?
4. What makes you come alive, brings you joy, fulfillment, and excitement?
5. Where do you add the greatest value?
6. How will you measure your life?

Noteworthy: Know why you want money.

7

"IF" AND "WHEN" WERE PLANTED, AND NOTHING GREW

"Action speaks louder than words but not nearly as often."

– Mark Twain

Your Survival Instinct at Work

You're probably reading this book because you have a compelling reason to seek financial freedom. And that search, having brought you here, will give you some insights to meet those "whys." When you know your "why," it flips a switch called passion, and that passion keeps you in pursuit of your goals long enough to find out how to achieve them.

Fear of failure causes us to want to know "how," but if you put the "how" first, you'll always be getting ready to get ready because one better idea after the next turns reasons of the heart into novelty. Eventually, you turn into one of those know-it-alls who don't have it all. If your "why" is big enough, you'll find your "how." And, we always find what our heart pursues.

Mark Twain said, "Action speaks louder than words, but not nearly as often." That's a great quote I believe to be true of most everyone, because our mindset is not set up for success. Have you ever gotten close to achieving something and then, for some reason, backed out because it just felt safer?

That's your survival instinct at work. You see, our brains are hardwired for survival, but the irony is that this survival instinct can sabotage your success.

You'll hear me often say that I help people find money they didn't think they had and save money they didn't think they could. There are so many ways I do that:

- The 20-day challenge
- The 30-day decree
- The round-up rule
- The 12-month maxim
- Intaxication
- The date precept

Not to mention showing you the exciting world of how to think for yourself. But as smart as good guidance may be, I've heard people say a three-letter word that, in a single breath, kills their chances of a great financial future: B-U-T. You can tell them something simple and virtuous like, "Save your money," and they say:

- But Social Security will take care of me.
- But I play the lottery.
- But my parents will leave me money.
- But I don't have enough to save.
- But my pension will take care of me.

- But I'm working on this idea to make more money... "Prestige Worldwide-wide-wide... Investors? Possibly you!" (*Step-Brothers*)

Look, "BUT" is an argument for our limitations, and when we argue for our limitations, we win. Remember, success and failure are not big events. They're a series of small decisions.

Noteworthy: Start now and stay consistent.

Hunter and Chase

To highlight the importance of starting now and staying consistent, I'd like to share a story about twin brothers named Hunter and Chase. Hunter and Chase were born as twin brothers. Their mother loved the idea of naming the first-born Hunter, and the one that followed she would name Chase, thinking that would be cute. By pure chance, they would get their pre-determined names.

As they grew, Hunter would start a project and work diligently for a short while, but Chase would get a later start and work hard to play catch-up. When they graduated high school, Hunter was quick to start saving $200/mo. Like so many times before, he would encourage Chase to do the same, but Chase wanted to spend money on clothes, dates, and travel. Eight years later, Hunter was able to influence Chase about saving the same amount in the same account he had.

Five years after Chase started saving, Hunter found the girl of his dreams, and they started a family. Of course, with new kids, a home, and more responsibilities, they justified never being able to save again.

Chase, who had originally started eight years late, felt bad about his youthful irresponsibility, so he made his mind up and was a diligent saver for the remainder of his working years.

When the brothers retired at age 65, they compared their account balances. Chase had always told Hunter to try and save again and often made him feel guilty when he didn't. So, Hunter didn't expect much, but he was surprised that his account had grown to $542,147. When Chase opened his account, he was pleased but confused why his $646,675 wasn't far more than Hunter's. Hunter had saved for a very short time early on, yet their ending balances were a lot closer than they'd imagined.

This story illustrates the power of the rule of 72. You may know this rule, which helps you figure out how many years it takes to double your money. For example, if you experience an average rate of 10% and divide that rate of return into 72, the answer will tell you how many years it will take for your money to double, in this case, 7.2 years.

If you focus only on the rate of return, you may miss the bigger issue, which is how many "doubles" you have in your lifetime. If you're 35 and plan on retiring at 65, most people do the math and figure they have 30 years. But that sounds like a long time, so it's easy to delay something as important as saving. A better way to look at it is that you have four doubles left. This helps to put time in sobering perspective.

Lights, Camera, Action!

You've probably heard the phrase "We don't plan to fail; we fail to plan." There is something to be said about taking action. I once heard that the UCLA School of Cinematography did a study years ago. The purpose of the study was to determine why male students were more successful in their movie careers relative to their female counterparts.

The conclusion was that while the gals were deeply discussing their plans and getting ready to get ready, the guys were out trying to make it happen. The guys had a lot of failures, many of which were embarrassing, but they moved forward nonetheless, chalking up success along the way.

Now, being male or female is a moot point. Money is blind to color, race, gender, and even intelligence, as was pointed out in the monkey story I shared earlier. The point here is: don't wait for it to "feel right." Improving your self-discipline means changing up your normal routine, which can be uncomfortable and awkward.

Charles Duhigg, author of *The Power of Habit*, explains that habitual behaviors have been traced to a part of the brain called the basal ganglia – a portion of the brain associated with emotions, patterns, and memories. Decisions, on the other hand, are made in the prefrontal cortex, a completely different area. When a behavior becomes a habit, we stop using our decision-making skills and instead function on autopilot.

Therefore, breaking a bad habit and building a new habit not only requires us to make active decisions, but it will also feel wrong. Think about how profound that is! Your brain will resist the change (even if it is for your own good). And it will resist this change in favor of what it has been programmed to do. The solution? Embrace the wrong. Acknowledge that it will take a while for your new regime to feel right, good, or natural. Keep chugging along. It *will* happen.

8

THE BIG LIE WE BUY

"It's better to live in the discomfort of your abilities than the comfort of your disabilities."

– Unknown

Have We Put the Cart before the Horse?

Years ago, investments and money management weren't a widespread concern. Dreyfus started advertising in 1957, but mainstream traction didn't seem to grab hold until the mid-90s. These days, it's all sport.

Now there is mass hysteria over what the stock markets did for the day. There's excitement if the market dropped by 1% or if it hit an all-time high. Commentators like Jim Cramer debrief America on what happened and what stocks they should be looking at, and you can hardly turn to an AM station on the weekends without hearing an advisor running some kind of "Safe Money" show. It's all turned into this force of nature that overwhelms us all.

The result is that public perception has changed. Tools are starting to replace asset management tasks that advisors used to perform. Free calculators are easily accessible, and information is so attainable that often the average person will bring up questions that the advisor has no immediate answer for. Because of this, financial advisors have become far less valuable in the public eye.

And touting better performance, cheaper insurance, or lower fees seems to be the go-to tactic these days for professionals.

Don't get me wrong. Insurance is important, as is money management, and we all want to have return on our money. But like Will Rogers so succinctly said, "I'm more interested in the return of my money than the return on my money." He wasn't ahead of his time; we have just gotten ahead of ourselves. In other words, we have placed the 10% of what's important regarding wealth-building (products and performance) in front of the 90% that's far more important (behavior and habit).

Three Circles and Three Squares

The problems we have had, have today, or will ever have with our finances will always be our problem. We should know and be prepared to take ownership of every decision we make. Having said that, there are forces out there that make it difficult to get ahead, and I want to address them.

Twenty-five years ago, 67% of all Americans were not prepared for retirement. Today that number is between 80 and 90%. As I've pointed out before, traditional financial services are broken.

When I started in the industry, I was taught how to sell one thing, a variable universal life policy, or VUL for short. We called the sales pitch the "three circles and three squares."

First, we'd have a discovery meeting to find out wants, needs, and what the prospect already had, like a home, life insurance, or savings accounts. Then we'd show the rule of 72, demonstrating the power of compound interest.

Next, we'd calculate whether they were on track to fund their retirement. Usually, there was a significant funding gap, and the moment their anxiety was highest about their financial future, we'd say, "You can save your money in an account earning 1%, 4%, or 12%. Which would you rather have?"

Of course, they'd say 12%. Then we'd say, "Now, there are different places that you can put your money, like CDs, annuities, and stocks, and each of them has different tax implications, so I'll ask you, what would you rather pay? Tax now, tax later, or tax never?"

Of course, they'd say tax never. Then we'd show them the holy grail of investing, aka the VUL.

The proposition was: "You buy a life policy that has a tax never status, it grows at 12% per year, and you get a free medical exam. How much did you say you wanted to invest each month?"

In other words, we had you right where we wanted you. Of course, I absolutely believed in what I was saying, as did the other 150,000 people selling the same thing. There was, and are today, a lot of so-called professionals doing the same sales dance; talk about weapons of mass destruction.

I'm a little dense, so it took me about four years to understand that this was not the best way to financially help people. And because I was good at it and made good money, it took me another two years before I made the decision to leave; shame on me.

Redemption: Going "Pro"

But I would redeem myself! I'd become a professional, go to the College for Financial Planning, take the eight-hour exam for the real license, and really help people. So, I did.

And as I sat in the lobby of the Merrill Lynch office on my first day of work, I thought, *Man, I've reached the zenith of my career. Now I'm a real financial professional.* As I walked around the office, I noticed all the advisors who were seasoned and tenured, the least of which for nearly 20 years, and I thought, *How impressive.*

At the time, managed accounts were becoming popular and seemed fair for clients, so I asked one of the older gentlemen how he felt about them, expecting he'd concur with my thoughts. His response gave me great clarity about the industry I worked in.

He said, "Why would I want to do that!? If I put a million dollars into a managed account, the client would pay 1% for the year, and I'd get paid a fraction of that.

"If I put them in bonds, I get paid 3%, and a year later, I can sell them out and make 3% and make another 3% when I buy them back into more bonds.

"And unless they look in the papers the next day, they think they've paid nothing for the transaction."

Before, we were hurting people because we were ignorant. But now? Now we were hurting people and knew it.

You're at the Bottom of the Food Chain

"It's easier to fool people than to convince them that they have been fooled."
– Mark Twain

Being completely sober about the above quote, in the next several pages, let me share with you what I know to be true. In the financial services industry, product manufacturers lie at the top of the food chain. They produce products like life insurance, mutual funds, managed portfolios, annuities, etc.

And the product purveyors? You guessed it, the financial professional. The licensed insurance agent, the stockbroker, even the so-called financial planner. I'm not saying there aren't really good professionals out there, but its slim pickings. Most of them learn a product or two very well, and many of the others operate with the best of intentions, but very, very few are true students of what they do.

Beware of people who give you their resume. I hear this all the time: "I've been in the business 20 years," or, "I've been in the business 30 years and have this paper hanging on my wall." Listen to me carefully. Many of them haven't been in the business 30 years, they've been in the business one year 30 times over.

I've been wealthy, lost it, and rebuilt, and on the ride up and down, I learned many things. One of these was that 90+% of what built my wealth was not a product or the performance of that product. It was tied to habits and behaviors that were developed over time.

Noteworthy: Being sold a financial product might make me poor.

A Value(less) Proposition

Pythagoras said numbers inevitably lead a person down the path of reason, but what if those numbers are flawed? When I started in financial services, mutual funds were not very well known, but they were just starting to make it to TV commercials en masse. This was when I learned of one of the largest funds at the time: Janus.

I also learned that Janus was a two-faced god. Looking back now, I think, *How ironic,* because the behavior of the financial services industry is often two-faced, like a contranym:

- Fast – you can move fast or stand fast
- Cleave – to split or join
- Garnish – to add a decorative touch or to take money from wages

Every quarter, these mutual funds do what's called window dressing. It's a strategy used to improve the appearance of a fund's performance before you see the reports. Basically, they're replacing losing stocks with winners, giving the appearance that they have wisdom and skill. It's a two-faced way of doing business, but it's necessary because they need to look good to sell shares.

Its agenda-driven marketing and is a means to get you to do things you normally wouldn't do. So, when you're in line at the grocery store and see that "XYZ" mutual fund picked all the winners for the year, you'll want to buy shares of that fund; this is right where they want you. We're bombarded with ads, marketing, salespeople, and the news and have relied on them as factual. If you knew the truth, you'd be beside yourself.

A Value(less) Proposition – Celebrities

This is where I make virtually everyone an enemy. Does a preface *really* matter here? Nope, so I'll dive right in.

I won't say his name, but it rhymes with "Behave Lousy." He believes only in term life insurance and 15-year mortgages, insists that you can average a 12% return over time, and believes all who disagree are stupid. He has a syndicated radio show, and he reaches the ears of a lot of people. But that doesn't make him right.

In fairness, he's not all bad. I appreciate:

- The way he is passionate about what he does.
- How he has made it his life's work to help people with money, because that is a root cause of a lot of other problems.
- The fact that he is unashamed of his relationship with God.

But there are eight issues I find peculiar or disagree with:

1. The envelope system – This system has been around virtually since the invention of the envelope in the 1800s and is referenced in newspapers of the time, like the *Evening World*. Today, it still works but is a little cumbersome and has proven for many to be a maintenance issue.

2. EveryDollar – This budget tool has many poor reviews on Play Store, but it also has good reviews. One thing is for sure: you will see a lot of bloggers and podcasters rave about it. However, they may very well be getting paid an affiliate fee, which encourages that. The tool is sharp and seems easy to use, but there is one big issue: forecasting.

The number one reason why most people get into financial trouble is that they spend and they don't know how that affects their budget by next payday, next month, etc. to be effective with your money, you need to be aware of the consequences at the moment you make a decision.

What you decide to use is important. There are two big reasons why it's best not to use technology that auto-populates banking activity:

- It isn't accurate all the time – You don't want to spend money that isn't there!
- Spending your money isn't a spectator sport – You need to be involved!

If you can't measure something, you can't understand it. If you can't understand it, you can't control it. If you can't control it, you can't improve it. And the right tools can put you in control and make managing and improving your budget a snap. When looking for an app, make sure the one you choose does the following:

- Features easy-to-input budget items by date and frequency.

- Enables you to account for interest earned on a bank account.
- Permits you to account for a percentage of your giving.
- Allows you to enter your income and expenses easily.
- Features a forecasting function so you know in the moment how your spending today impacts your finances days down the road.
- Can give you reports.

Then decide which is best for your family and stick to it.

3. Baby steps – I disagree with the order in which he lists his seven baby steps, but the most glaring issue, particularly for a faith-based company, is their underlying pattern:

STEP 1: Save $1,000 for ME.
STEP 2: Pay off all MY debt.
STEP 3: Create an emergency fund for ME.
STEP 4: Invest 15% for MY future.
STEP 5: Save for MY kids.
STEP 6: Pay off MY house.
STEP 7: Build wealth for MY family and – dead last, almost as if it were an afterthought – giving.

Whether you are a person of faith or not, giving is one of the most important first steps you can take to building wealth. Whatever our religious (or otherwise) affiliation, where we put our money is a testament to our faith. From a purely secular standpoint, the baby steps still have issues that make little sense:

STEP 1: Save $1,000 (this is the same as step 3).

STEP 2: Pay off all debt (except the house) using the debt snowball (snowball is not the most mathematically efficient and may not be the most emotionally efficient).

STEP 3: Create an emergency fund (same as step 1).

STEP 4: Invest 15% into a Roth IRA and pre-tax vehicles (15% may or may not be the right amount for you).

STEP 5: Save for kid's college education using tax-favored plans (they might not go to college).

STEP 6: Pay off the house early (same as step 2, and 15-year mortgage is the expensive route – challenge me).

STEP 7: Build wealth and give (even if you are an atheist, the giving part of all seven steps should be first)

4. He is adamant about 12% returns – As a retired investment advisor who has actually managed a handful of portfolios, I can tell you that no professional will consistently produce 12% returns per year, especially over the 20- and 30-year periods that he uses to excite people about the growth of their money. This is

misleading, and the American family deserves better than that because it can lead to a false sense of security.

5. Zander insurance – Zander is the sole recommendation for insurance. One of the reasons I love financial coaching is because pushing products is the reason the American people are no better today than 25 years ago. It's not about the products, and when you push a relationship with a product or a carrier of products, you can't escape the bias that exists.

6. The ELP network (endorsed local providers) – This is where he charges financial professionals a large amount per month in return for giving them *you* as a lead. The most peculiar part is that he claims that he tests the local providers' hearts before they are allowed to pay him money to receive you as a lead. In my humble opinion, there are two things wrong with that:

   a. No one yet has come up with a way to truly know someone's heart.

   b. Even if this person you were referred to has a good heart, they get paid at the end of the day to push products, whether insurance, annuities, or portfolios, and those often cost you a lot more than you think.

7. He is adamant about the 15-year mortgage – Everyone has their own financial fingerprint, which is why I emphasize learning how to think through these issues. Making a mistake here could cost the average person over $100,000.

8. He is seemingly always adamant – If you have watched any videos or heard him on the radio, you'll know he takes such a hard stand on something that the other person can't possibly be right, even a little. In his responses, they are either in agreement with him or they are stupid. Life and people's situations are complex, and not everything is so straightforward that unless you do a thing, it's "stupid."

He is good at helping people with their budgets and debt, and I hope he continues with much success. I also appreciate that he puts God first, and I am happy to see that he has that part of his life in perspective.

However, Christians can be fallible, often even more so than good people that don't go to church or think of themselves as Christians. To place so much emphasis on God can make people feel uncomfortable. It's also possible that he's using God as a way to ingratiate himself with one of the largest marketplaces in America. I hope that's not the case. But again, we don't know the heart of a man.

A Value(less) Proposition – Financial Advisors

Today's advisor proposition, "Give me all your money, pay me to manage it, and in five years, we'll see if that was the right decision," has investors bouncing from one advisor that doesn't live up to expectations to the next advisor willing to charge less.

Trying to do the right job, advisors give you a profile test to identify what your risk tolerance is. If you aren't on track for retirement (like 80–90% of our population) then they lay out these options:

1. Save more money now.
2. Get a second job.
3. Retire later.

4. Work part-time in retirement.
5. Accept a lower lifestyle in retirement.

None of these are desirable, so there is a checkmate (in a sense) that leaves you with the one option that seems the easiest (like taking a magic pill for a headache).

That option is buying into the next portfolio that has a higher historical return. After all, you answered the profile questions, and therefore, the new portfolio must be right for you; this is right where they want you.

Then the market drops by 10%, and you fire your advisor and take another profile (forgetting the answers they gave five years ago on the last profile) with a new ambitious advisor who runs you through the same process. Of course, you'll fire that advisor in five years for being too conservative in a bounce-back market. When money moves, money is made, and the chief goal for these advisors is adding to AUM (assets under management). They do this by selling a new portfolio that had better performance than your current portfolio over the last one, three, five, or ten years. They may even reduce your fee.

This process has caused advisors to be viewed as a commodity, which should be scary to both them and you because it leads to an endless rinse-and-repeat cycle that accomplishes little more than angst. Sooner or later, investors will find a way around all this, with or without the aid of the advisor. I'm hoping this book, if not the catalyst, is the impetus.

A Value(less) Proposition – Insurance Agents

"Buy the S&P 500 guaranteed to not lose money with a free medical exam, and in twenty years, we'll see if it hasn't imploded." This was a proposition that morphed from whole-life and split-annuity tactics as new products like VUL (variable universal life), FIA (fixed indexed annuities), and EIUL (equity-indexed universal life) arrived in the 90s.

Today it doesn't seem to have changed much. Insurance and annuity agents are pushing their products as equity alternatives. There are issues with this that become clear as a client experiences them many years after the sale. If the marketing of equities products plays on greed, fixed products play on fear. That play on fear is powerful, and it will be even more so in the troubled world to come.

So, the client is placed in a long-term product where they think they are covered, and because there is little to no incentive to deal with the relationship financially, the agent moves on to the next prospect, proposing the same thing.

Because of the estranged relationship, the investor meets with another advisor. The new advisor explains to them that the contract they have will implode. Coming to the rescue, the advisor restructures the contract, or the cash value is processed as a 1035 exchange into a variable annuity.[9]

There is one main question: Who was making sure the recommendation was right, the advisor or the agent? There is a solid case for both sides, but who made sure it was optimal (holistically speaking)?

---

[9] A 1035 exchange is a provision in the tax code that allows you, as a policyholder, to transfer funds from a life insurance, endowment, or annuity to a new policy without having to pay taxes.

Behavioral finance might exist (in part) because of the ongoing heated debate from opposing industries.[10] Maybe it's time we take a look at a different kind of behavioral finance, the kind that requires us to look at ourselves.

The Battle Pushing Investors Away

While the pros are busy jockeying for position, average people have something else on their minds. Something is happening in your hearts that professionals are seemingly unaware of. The effort to fight for meals creates confusion, which is pushing you away from them. Confused people don't buy, and the traditional financial services industry has collectively confused the marketplace. Average people are starting to believe that all of this is a lie (as outlined in Chapter 1).

If you look at the issue from a 30,000-foot view, you can see that there are virtues to both propositions and that at the end of the day, every financial instrument exists for a

---

[10] Behavioral finance is the study of the influence of psychology on the behavior of investors. It focuses on the fact that investors are not always rational, have limits to their self-control, etc.

purpose. Furthermore, I think few would disagree with the idea that very little of your ultimate wealth in life is derived from the activities of advisors pushing the next product or portfolio. Money management, timing of buying and selling (whether securities or an insurance product), and selection of money managers are the white noise obscuring something far more important.

If you search Google for "The most important behaviors to building wealth," you'd be hard pressed to find information to the contrary. No blog, news article, or white paper I found names an investment product as the primary reason someone amassed and kept wealth. So, why is there so much professional focus on those things?

Most of the wealth we will ever amass in life will come from behavior, habits, and making decisions that have known positive impacts on our finances. If the basics of building wealth are things like charitable giving, paying yourself first, being free of debt, and careful decision-making, then it stands to reason that this activity needs accountability. It needs to be planned in advance and revisited regularly and in such a way that makes it clear how each decision impacts your financial life.

To say that the failure to do this is the advisor's fault is not entirely fair. Advisors need the proper:

- Tools
- Incentive
- Environment

They need these things so they can be the financial "thinkers" the general public needs them to be. They need:

- Efficient back/front office technology
- Enterprise systems
- Professional management and processes

They also need financial planning software capable of constructing a quality plan in a timely fashion – not retirement planning, but bona fide financial planning that proves they exercised a fiduciary process in a category-iterative fashion and provided the most optimal advice for your future.

Not having the tools and systems in place is onerous in and of itself. Throw in the ever-tightening regulations they face, and a bad attitude will follow. And we all know where that gets us. I wrote extensively on this in my book *The Unrivaled Advisor*, where I outlined how advisors can operate a more efficient and profitable practice while doing the right thing for their clients.

The financial services industry can help if its perspective changes. The middle and lower classes and "income rich, asset poor" are grossly underserved by advisors, and there are few who have the desire to champion this cause.

Standing in the way of this desire is an environment-driven perspective from the financial services industry. Previously, I shared some reasons that should change these professionals' opinions:

- The middle class needs help more than the wealthy.
- Advisors are ambassadors. Bringing goodwill to the public leads to a satisfying career.
- When helped, people become raving fans, and an army of advocates makes the experience viral.

The challenge inherent to each point above is:

1. At the very top of the food chain are manufacturers. These are the companies that manufacture the

products built for profit after the advisor is paid. These products need to be sold, and to sell a product, whether insurance or a portfolio, there is really only one way for an advisor to make an honest profit these days: by volume, either the size of the client's assets (the wealthy) or the number of clients served (the middle class). To serve the middle class, independent financial advisors have to operate like a real business that is structured and efficient.

Yet the proposition, people, and automation strategies required to make that work at the independent advisor level are virtually non-existent (read *The Unrivaled Advisor* for a full understanding). Therefore, the propensity to gravitate to the wealthy for sales is extremely hard to argue against. This leads to the second challenge.

2. If survivable profit that serves the middle class doesn't exist, it's likely that the advisor engages in questionable or outright predatory selling. In fact, FINRA (The regulatory body that oversees advisors) saw a record-breaking year for advisor fines in 2016 of $176 million,

up 87% from the previous year. This is astonishing given the fact that over nine years, from 2008–2016 (a stock market recovery period), there were 12,398 disciplinary actions, with 727 advisors suspended and 517 barred from practicing altogether in 2016 alone.[11] When a small business isn't efficient and saddled with heavy regulation, it has to make up for it, usually through questionable selling practices, making it hard for new advisors to survive or enter the field.

As the industry purges advisors for misconduct and tightens the rules in response to lawsuits, the industry's focus is turned to solving the problem of the middleman (the advisor). Cutting the middleman reduces the trouble but also removes the human element required for Americans to get true help. People don't do business with companies; they do business with people because people are relatable.

---

[11] https://us.eversheds-sutherland.com/NewsCommentary/Press-Releases/197511/Annual-Eversheds-Sutherland-Analysis-of-FINRA-Cases-Shows-Record-Breaking-2016.

3. This all causes an industry that could be thriving to instead age and shrink – along with the financial success of the American household. Forgetting one's duty as an ambassador leads to a widespread negative view from middle America, which leaves you to fend for yourself when it comes to making the right financial decisions.

Like I said earlier, if people aren't educated and cared for, they become adversarial, which manifests itself into movements that elect officials whose constituents insist on higher taxes for the wealthy and free health care, not to mention activism like Occupy Wall Street. This affects all of us by creating a deeper social divide and breeds ignorance that erodes what would otherwise be a great marketplace.

It seems unlikely that such a large industry so set in its ways can deliver what is really needed for the American family. With such a cost of money and time, any proposed project would be deemed unreasonable. Meanwhile, Americans are desperate for help. Unfortunately, I believe it's too late for traditional financial services. Fortunately, where there is a void, it will be filled, and this void is being filled by financial coaches.

Having given others a name, it's easy to give myself one, too. I suppose that with all the stories I've shared about my misadventures, I could be called "Been Gluttonous." This book and the many other compiled works that are called "UGRU" stem from my epiphanies over a quarter-century. Some arrived slower than they probably should have. Nevertheless, they all make a case for financial coaching.

The Case for Financial Coaching

To realize financial success as a household, there must be six basic actions.

1. **Learn.** Learning can take any form these days, from listening to a recording, watching a video, or sitting in on training, but the important part is that there must be a place where the benefits of learning can be enjoyed.

2. **Internalize.** It is not enough to simply fill your head with information. To be effective with that information, you need to internalize what you take in. In other words, it must be meaningful to you. When the information you take in resonates at a deep level, this will flip your passion switch on. And as you may have experienced,

when you are passionate about something, you want to tell people about it. This is the important spark that becomes a person's "why." And that activity leads to not only the fulfillment, but the sustainment of behavioral change.

3. **Teach.** Once you have gained a passion for what you have learned, the third element is to teach. We have all been told that the teacher is always the one who learns more, and this is critical because the only way to sustain a behavior change long term is to help others achieve what you have. This step is so vital that it's listed as the 12th and final step in Alcoholics Anonymous.

4. **Goals.** Without goals, your household is like a ship without a rudder, going in circles until one day crashing on the rocks. People need an environment to put the exercise of setting goals front and center. After all, you can't hit a target that doesn't exist.

5. **Plans.** Plans are the vehicles allowing you to reach your goals. If you follow them, they will care for your goals. You should clearly define the "how" now that you have your "why."

6. **Accountability:** Without accountability, all goals and plans would be made in vain. I'm not talking about portfolio reviews or measuring portfolio expectations to stated goals. Accountability lies in the client's behavior because this is where the vast majority of wealth is built. People need someone they can give absolute latitude to hold them accountable.

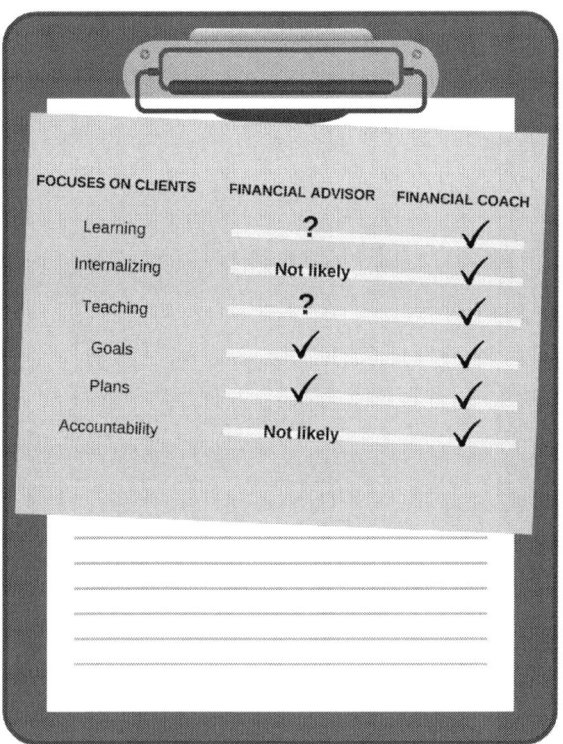

So, it stands to reason that the answer does not lie in a product or a rate of return per se but in behavior that brings us to an alternative solution. It's important to find a place where learning, internalization, empowerment to teach others, and accountability are all championed. Doing this brings enormous value to the American household and its finances.

Many of these areas are not looked after when a commission or a fee as a percentage of investable assets is part of the equation, because the perceived work is over once the transaction is complete and energy is reserved for gaining new accounts. Financial coaching can bridge this gap.

Financial coaching places a focus on the critical areas that are needed for real change to take place and are in a unique position to solve the great household financial crisis that has plagued our nation since the advent of credit.

Coaching is the second-fastest-growing industry in the world. With just under two thousand coaches in the United States serving approximately 50,000 families, financial coaching is the most nascent sector of the coaching industry, but its impact cannot be denied.[12] Despite the early stages of this new industry and lack of standardized programs, training, and measurements, the outcomes are very promising:

- 72% increased net income
- 48% increased net worth
- 44% increased credit score (median increase of 39 points)

According to *Forbes*, the coaching industry is booming and generates $1 billion per year in the United States alone,[13] a 35% increase from 2011 to 2015.[14] This is a strong indicator of what's to come with financial coaching and points to how receptive Americans are when it comes to coaching. I believe Americans are tired of blindly listening to the experts and getting burned. They are tired of being sold a

---

[12]https://www.kansascityfed.org/publications/community/connections/articles/2017/q12017/financial_coaching.

[13]https://www.forbes.com/sites/ashleystahl/2016/04/25/busting-the-top-5-myths-about-the-coaching-industry/#6b/c5c424491.

[14] coachfederation.org/2016study.

product, and they are tired of overpaying for a service that underdelivers.

I believe Americans are ready for financial knowledge that empowers them to make informed decisions, covers all the main issues they will face in their financial world, and arms them with the necessary knowhow and emotional capacity. There are many alternatives out there, but in my opinion, they pale in comparison to financial coaching.

In medical terms, the alternatives are hemorrhaging. Going a different route leaves you with learning through trial by fire. And unless you're a professional student, that's not the way you want to go about building real and lasting financial change. Not to mention that the alternatives can be far more expensive, ranging from tens to hundreds of thousands of dollars more.

	COACHING	ADVISORS	AGENTS	WEB SEARCH
IMMEDIATE NEEDS				
Learn to Budget	✓	NO	✓	?
Stop surprises thru organization	✓	NO	NO	?
Stop feeling insecure	✓	NO	NO	NO
Focus on immediate struggles	✓	NO	NO	?
Save money you didn't think	✓	?	NO	?
Find money you didn't think	✓	NO	NO	?
COACHING				
Answers & Resources now	✓	✓	✓	?
Master you mindset	✓	NO	NO	NO
Accountability	✓	NO	NO	NO
Debt	✓	NO	NO	NO
Planning*	?	?	?	NO
FOUNDATIONAL KNOWLEDGE				
Debt	✓	NO	NO	?
Financial Calculator	✓	NO	NO	?
Planning*	?	?	?	NO
Insurance	✓	NO	✓	?
Retirement	✓	✓	✓	?
PRODUCT AGNOSTIC				
Insurance	✓	NO	NO	✓
Annuities	✓	NO	NO	✓
Stocks/Bonds	✓	NO	NO	✓
Mutual Funds	✓	NO	NO	✓

*Coaches should only aid clients with guided self-discovery unless properly licensed for financial planning

---

[15] Coaches should only aid clients with guided self-discovery unless properly licensed for financial planning.

A Value(less) Proposition – Google, YouTube, etc.

You might think free is great! So, what about Google and YouTube? With all the information the web contains, it still offers a grave lack of instruction on how to execute. How can you possibly collect all the conflicting data that exists about your money on the internet and make decisions based on it? The answer is you can't, but coaching can. So, to answer the question "Why me when it's free?" Let's start with:

- **Results vs. random info** – Succinct information is giving you the best chance to succeed.

- **Raw info is not enough** – Let's say I gave you my phone number in raw data form. You wouldn't be able to call me, right? But if I gave you that data in the proper sequence, you could call me.

- **It's what you don't know you don't know** – You're not being told what you could search on Google. You're being told what you didn't think to search.

- **It's not the availability; it's the ability** – Searching, weighing conflicting points, and not knowing who is right makes synthesizing that info nearly impossible. Even if you did have the time, do you really want to spend it on that? Or do you want to live your life doing more enjoyable things?

- **Easier and probably *far* cheaper** – Never mind the costly mistakes; what about your time? If you searched collectively for one hour a day (five minutes here, ten minutes there) for one year and you earned $20 per hour, it would cost you $7,300 to get that quote/unquote "free" information, not to mention the brain-numbing tedium of the search.

  A great video that drives that point home is "What the Internet Is Doing to Our Brains."[16] It's only a few minutes long and is really good!

- **Support, accountability, and motivation** – You can learn all day by reading on the net. You can share and like info all day long, and that might feel good, too. You can set goals and make plans around that, but if you don't have a coach, you're missing support,

---

[16] https://www.youtube.com/watch?v=cKaWJ72x1rI.

accountability, and motivation. Ahhhh, the missing ingredient, my support network! Free is fine, but a good coach is way better than free! It's not about whether you can afford a coach. The reality is: you cannot afford to *not* have a coach.

The last and probably the most important reason to use a financial coach is synthesis.

Synthesis: Your Key to Thrive

Just because data is available doesn't mean its correct. I've got a question: is carbon dioxide important? It's critical, right? Without carbon dioxide, there would be no plants, and without plants, we humans would have long since passed. Why? Because plants have an amazing ability to perform photosynthesis, which converts carbon dioxide to oxygen.

Think about it this way. When the professionals talk about finance, what comes out of their mouths? Carbon dioxide.

These words (like CO_2 to plants) are the building blocks to your ability to thrive. But like plants, your ability to synthesize is key. The question is, how do you synthesize that information for your own benefit?

Last time I checked, when you search Google for "personal finance," there are 1.8 billion results. And statistics tell us that 90% of the search results people pick are on the first page. My point here is that the quality of content rarely makes the first page. What makes the first page is simply the best marketed. As you know, you are being marketed to around the clock. It all sounds so good and so smart, and it's right where they want your mind to be. In the world of personal finance, this is often not a great as you think.

9

YOUR FINANCIAL PLAN IS LIKELY WRONG

"Prescription without diagnosis is malpractice."

– Unknown

What Financial Planning Is Not

I am surprised to have run across so many advisors who seem to mix up the terminology on this, so I felt it important to cover what financial planning is and what it isn't. Financial planning has little to do with portfolios and their allocation, and a true financial plan is devoid of incorporating portfolios (though it does include the assets themselves) and Monte Carlo simulations in planning software.[17] The software, in most cases, does not fully comply with FINRA Rule 2214, anyway.[18]

All of this is more retirement planning, where they would determine goals, identify total income, deduct expenses, and implement a portfolio that they would then manage toward the end goal that had originally been set. This is a highly problematic approach for nearly anyone because it lures all parties involved down this road that ultimately

---

[17] Such simulations show possible outcomes of portfolio decisions and assess the impact of risk, allowing for better decision-making under uncertainty.

[18] http://finra.complinet.com/en/display/display.html?rbid=2403&element_id=10651.

prevents critical financial issues from being identified. The essence of the relationship ends up in a vicious cycle. What unfolds through this is the process I described in the advisor value proposition: Give me all your money, pay me to manage it, and in five years, we'll see if that was a good decision. That process looks like the familiar doctor visit:

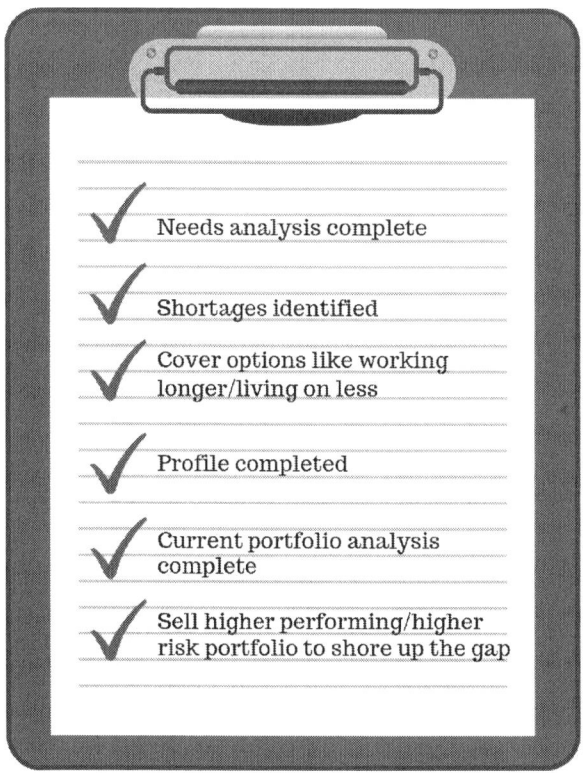

Magic show complete. This is investment planning methodology, not financial planning.

What Holistic Financial Planning Is

Holistic financial planning is all-encompassing. It is a process that considers all aspects of the financial household and will likely require a quarterback or a guide, someone like an advisor or the right coach to guide you with the proper software as a self-discovery process (think TurboTax).

Someone must take the lead of your aggregate picture so that the decisions made are the most optimal relative to every other nuanced financial element. In the end, one thing matters more than anything, and that is to have a clear picture of where you stand and where you are going no matter where you are in your financial journey.

The only way to accomplish this is through:

- Establishing goals
- Identifying current resources
- Identifying current courses of action

Then go through a category-Iterative process on each current and possible financial decision in all the following areas (though not necessarily limiting yourself to these):

- Investment real estate
- Primary residence
- Debt structure
- Estate planning
- Tax planning
- College planning
- Distribution planning
- Alternative investments
- Business planning

The end goal is to identify and ultimately provide the most optimal result. Of course, all decisions should be within the parameter of what is acceptable to you.

Why Holistic Financial Planning matters

My first car was a 1976 Dodge Colt, and it came equipped with a two-stage carburetor, which was fun, and bias ply tires, which were also fun, but in a different way. They were far less stable on the road than today's radials, but they were great in the dirt, and I had a blast driving them off-road. Living in Phoenix as a teenager, we were never far from a desert road, and boy, did my friends and I put our cars through their paces.

One thing I always remembered was a good bit of advice that probably saved me from catastrophe: when driving a vehicle that is out of control on the road, hold the wheel as straight as possible, let off the gas pedal, and do not press the brake. This made a lot of sense, and I can say (from experience) that it works.

That's the way I see today's process with clients, only the advice they are receiving is to oversteer, slam on the brakes, or press the accelerator. The investing public is starting to see that advisors and their advice are just as foolish as a driver doing the same thing in a vehicle. When we stop short of real holistic planning, the picture is seriously skewed, and pushing down on the accelerator leads to all the same outcomes of doing the same thing in a car that is out of control.

Let me explain. Let's say there are two clients, each age 65. They are identical in every way possible. They have the same:

- Accounts and fees
- Rate of returns
- Beginning balances and cost basis on each account[19]
- Income needs and duration
- Inflation rate
- Tax brackets

So, they have the same financial outcome, right? Wrong. Client #1 had a shortfall at age 89. Client #2 had a sustained retirement through age 90 and still had $652,000 left over. When accounting for the money required to fund Client #1 in their last year, the total difference is $764,000. This was accomplished by calculating the most optimal distribution order among each investment.

The main point of this exercise is this: the $764,000 extra is equivalent to a 50% return on the beginning liquid net worth of $1.5 million. Do the math, and that equates to a 2%-per-year rate of return for 26 years where you didn't have to rely on a higher-performing investment.

---

[19] Cost basis is the original value of an asset for tax purposes. This value is used to determine the capital gain, which is equal to the difference between the asset's cost basis and the current market value.

In other words, we don't have to push the accelerator when we find that client #1 has a shortfall; we just have to rework the distribution. There is no way you could have known this without first exercising your planning muscles.

Incorporating how you hold debt, pension maximization, time-segmented distribution, mortgage acceleration, stretch IRAs, Roth conversions, and many more planning strategies into one holistic plan is the only way to plan properly.

Therefore, it's important to control what you can and manage what you can't. If you can control the aspects of fees, taxes, and other decisions that have a positive known outcome, this will translate into a return on money. Then, and only then, is it time to consider investment selection.

Where planning counts most

It's been said that the most dangerous part of climbing Mt. Everest is not in the ascent, but in the downhill journey. The closer to retirement you are, the more significant planning becomes. Chasing returns (not that it ever was the most important thing) is definitely not at the top of the list.

It's when the downhill journey begins, i.e., retirement, that planning (not that it wasn't important before) is imperative. This is where the consideration of financial decisions and distribution planning requires the utmost focus. And just like any Mt. Everest excursion, this process is best addressed with a knowledgeable guide – and, I might add, a guide with the proper tools.

Performance is far more complex than just evaluating the return on a portfolio. It also involves safeguarding your portfolio in down economies, steering through sideways markets, and making decisions today that ultimately affect your financial standing tomorrow.

Everyone has their own financial fingerprint, yet almost 70% of client market share is fought over by advisors who arm themselves on the unknown basis of manager performance and fees, further commoditizing the financial services industry.[20] This all begs the question: how

---

[20] Cerulli Associates and College for Financial Planning, 2009 Survey of Trends in the Financial Planning Industry.

thorough is your planning process? This question includes your philosophy as well as the tools you use to support it.

Problems with today's planning philosophy

"Control what you can; manage what you can't."

– Unknown

There are two big issues I see with today's planning philosophy: lack of proper iterative planning and the way historical performance is viewed.

Lack of Category-Iterative Planning

The only way to produce a proper financial plan is to go through a category-iterative process, where your financial life is separated into major categories, like real estate, estate planning, asset distribution, tax planning, etc.

Once each category is identified, an iterative process should begin whereby you employ tactics that achieve a different outcome in the ending net worth value of the plan as a whole. From this process, the most optimal ending trajectory is identified per category and applied to the plan holistically.

The next natural step would be to move on to the next category and apply the same iterative process relative to the new category, being mindful that the most optimal iteration in one category might adversely affect the previous optimization of another category. This process can be difficult and time-consuming, so having the right technology and tools is extremely important.

This is the only way for planners to truly act as a fiduciary for you, and it is what is expected of every advisor today. However, a completely different philosophy is routinely exercised, as I have outlined earlier:

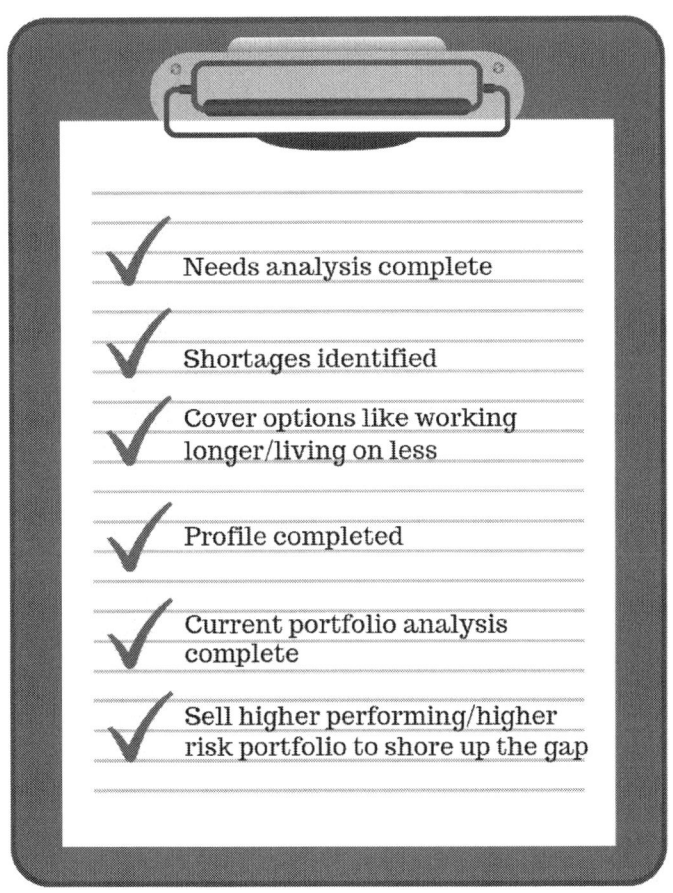

Even worse, the philosophy is exercised through a particular historical performance lens.

Long Term Isn't Long Enough

"It's hard to see things when you're too close. Take a step back and look."

– Bob Ross, artist

I remember sitting in a seminar in 2003 that an advisor was giving, and he showed the audience a chart of market performance by decade, starting with the Great Depression. He reasoned with the audience that there was, in fact, only one losing decade, which he referred to as both an aberration and an event that was a hundred-year phenomenon, like a hundred-year flood.

The decade he was talking about was the 70s, and he went on to explain that there has never been a sliding ten-year period since or before. Of course, no data was provided before the Great Depression.

I never really thought much about it until late 2007. I had been running five portfolios in my RIA, and I was frustrated that I could not find positive indicators for constructing the portfolios going into 2008. In fact, I was so frustrated that I placed 100% of my clients in cash equivalents that year except for those in an income portfolio. By the end of the year, four things had happened:

1. I lost ten million in assets mid-year from clients who had left me because they weren't happy with my decision.
2. Saving the clients that stayed from doom, I waved the banner for all I could get and wound up bringing in another 50 million with new investors.
3. I decided that my portfolio management days were over because I realized that I was human and my decision could have been a HUGE mistake.
4. I became intensely interested in researching the markets before the Great Depression.

On the fourth point, I found something that was very interesting. I realized that during the 1800s, each decade or so had a rather large loss. Back then, they referred to these as "panics," but the pattern of suffering losses as much as 50% each decade came to an end with the Great Depression.

When advisors use the Great Depression as a starting point, I believe it skews the picture because, for nearly five decades after the Great Depression, we had unprecedented prosperity. This ended in 1973 with the oil embargo, which hit a whole new generation with back-to-back market losses greater than 50%. Twenty-seven years later, we experienced the tech bubble, with back-to-back-to-back losses of 50%. Then, seven years after that, the real estate bubble burst, and again we faced this 50% loss in back-to-back markets.

The philosophy that advisors have viewed the markets through and sold you on, I believe, is myopic. I don't believe the "aberration" was the decade of the 70s. I think the aberration was the unprecedented prosperity for fifty years after the Great Depression. The pattern seems clear to me now that we have seen these 50% losses occur with greater frequency in the last 45 years, and in my opinion, we are going back to the norm of the 1800s, where we should be expecting a shakeout every decade or so.

Looking at the next chart, you can easily see the market drawdowns for the one hundred years before the Great Depression were far more active than our modern markets.

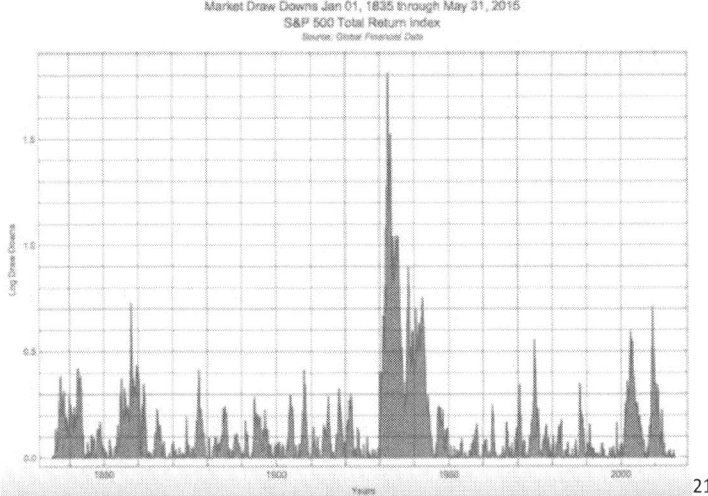
[21]

If you think the past is irrelevant and does not apply in today's modern era, I would ask: at what point does history hit the "modern" mark? Modern computers weren't around during the Great Depression, the internet wasn't around in the 80s, and smartphones weren't around at the change of the millennium.

I would contend that behavior is at the root of the trading system and that more data does not mean better market

---

[21] Ben Carlson. "180 Years of Market Drawdowns" April 24, 2016. http://awealthofcommonsense.com/2016/04/180-years-of-market-drawdowns/.

behavior. In fact, it could mean quite the opposite. So, I would say the second issue is that advisors and other well-known personalities are too bullish on future returns, especially as applied to financial plans.

Most advisors I speak with say they use relatively low returns when modeling their client plan and feel comfortable with that, but this could prove disastrous. I explain why in the next few pages, under "Static Returns."

Problems with Today's Planning Software

For the last 11 years of my career, financial planning was my signature service, but finding planning software proved way too difficult. Some were really cool looking and had very professional user interfaces, but they seriously lacked the ability to do some heavy lifting on planning. Some software didn't even show the difference between tax-deferred and tax-free returns.

I ultimately used software that was open architecture, but I about wore the buttons out on my HP 12C (financial calculator) because it just lacked a lot of functionality. I would spend from six to as much as forty hours constructing a quality plan because of this, but I could show an accurate and detailed plan, and that was a priority for my clients and me.

I am not the only one to observe that planning software is ineffective. This is what the Society of Actuaries had to say:

> *According to a report by the Society of Actuaries (SOA), the majority of available planning software tools still fail to effectively address the wide range of individual issues related to retirement.*
>
> *The SOA analyzed 12 financial planning software programs most commonly used by individuals and financial advisors which were available over the internet or designed for use by professional advisors.*
>
> *After crunching the numbers in the twelve programs, the Society of Actuaries found that planning software needs to better address key planning issues including: Longevity, unexpected events and risks, housing, social security and annuities.*[22]

More recently, Michael Kitces weighed in on this when he said: "The ability to illustrate specific planning strategies, or

---

[22] *The Network Journal* article from 2-15-2011 by Robert Powell.

the impact of various financial services products as a solution, has remained remarkably limited."[23]

I could write another book dedicated to just the shortfalls in planning, but to briefly expand on this thought, I will cover two huge and common issues revolving around the use of static returns and Monte Carlo simulation in plans.

Static Returns

When I was in my third year of college math, I remember getting into a very interesting debate over standard deviation. My contention was that advisors (me being one) were assigning static rates to accounts in our planning process and that this couldn't possibly be serving the client well. I also believed this was likely causing an inaccurate accounting of future projections, though, to what extent, I was unsure.

My professor quickly responded that it was irrelevant how volatile any account was as long as the mean (average) was

---

[23] www.kitces.com/blog/designing-the-financial-planning-software-of-the-future-calculator-collaboration-tool-and-client-pfm/.

equal to the static return used in the plan. However, one simple question threw a monkey wrench into what was, of course, mathematical fact.

That question was: so, what happens to the trajectory of account values when we treat income needed each year as a variable? This has been part of my life's work, which is illustrated in a few pages, so let me set the stage for what you will see.

Investment outcomes in the real world are the result of a near-infinite set of variables, but advisors should try to create the most real-to-life scenario for you as possible by including the testing of what I refer to as "market dynamics."

Market dynamics are compared to the static returns commonly used by advisors in the examples I use. I have found that the assumptions of static returns can lead to a false sense of confidence as it relates to a client's future because they create a perfect scenario. I believe that by using a past market that is dynamic in nature, you can more closely align future expectations.

This is done by taking a stretch of historical performance data (like S&P 500 performance from 1970–2014) and overlaying each year through the course of your expected returns. In other words, the performance of 1970 becomes the illustrated performance of your first year of the plan, and so on. If the illustrated plan happens to be longer in years than that of the historical data, the original first year of performance then picks up where the data leaves off.

For example, you illustrate 30 years in your plan but choose to use performance data from 2000–2009. In this case, the 11th year of the plan uses the performance of the year 2000 again and continues as it did in the first cycle.

The reports shown on the next few pages are identical (meaning they are the same client) except for the comparison of a static vs. a dynamic environment. The static rates are derived from the same average return found in the dynamic period, which is illustrated separately and comparatively.

All other numbers in each scenario are equal, including fees, inflation rates, beginning account balances, withdrawal rates, tax brackets, and distribution order of each account, so they are compared static against a dynamic environment.

The first chart you see shows average returns (dividends included) in each year of 12.02% (CAGR[24] = 10.49%) with a standard deviation of 17.47%. This is the identical average performance (dividends included) of the S&P 500 from 1970 to 2014.[25]

---

[24] Compound annual growth rate (CAGR) is a business and investing specific term for the geometric progression ratio that provides a constant rate of return over the time period.

[25] http://www.moneychimp.com/features/market_cagr.htm.

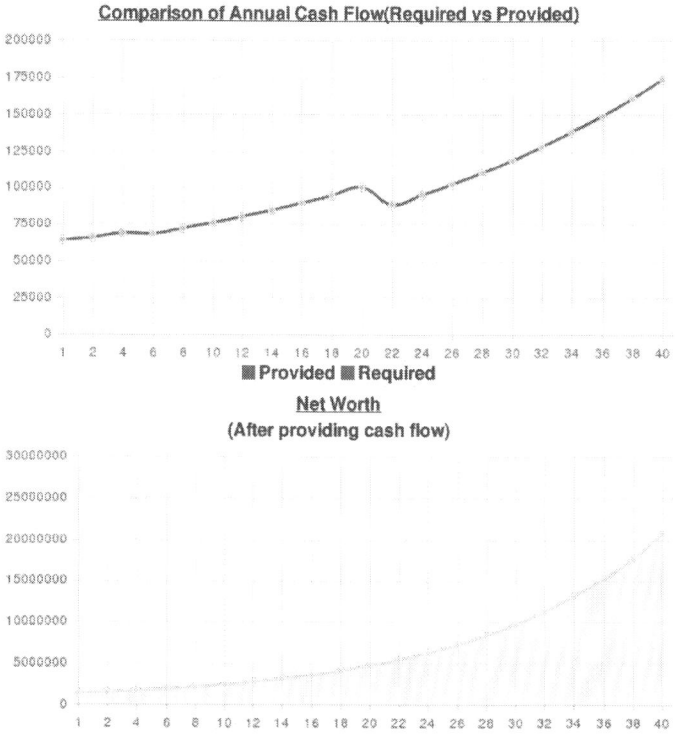

As you can see, the resulting net worth is over $20 million, which would certainly warrant estate planning like a QPRT (qualified personal residence trust) and/or an ILIT (irrevocable life insurance trust). As fun as this sounds to those who offer legal advice or sell insurance, let's see what happens when we add the impact of the market dynamics overlay on the next chart.

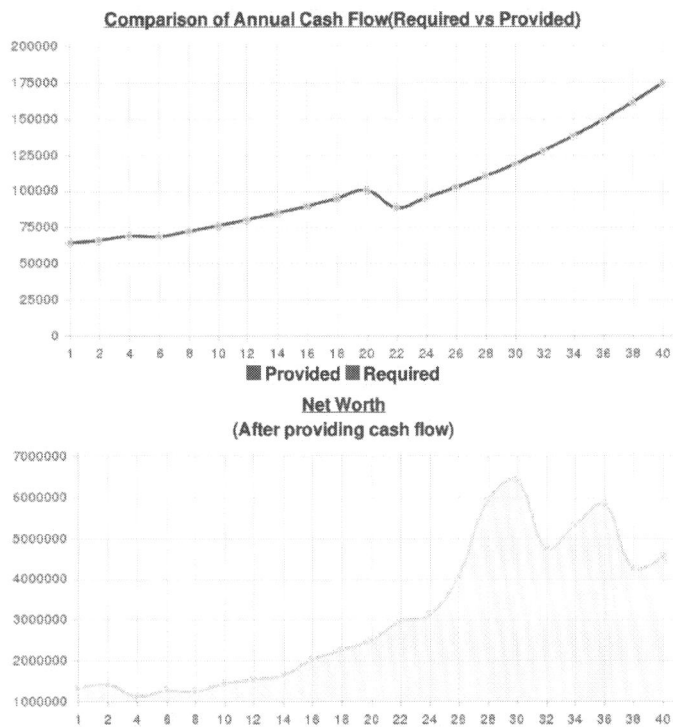

The outcome is dramatic even though the same average return exists in the mix. Now you have an ending net worth less than $5 million, which doesn't even exceed the available unified credit equivalent by today's Internal Revenue Code (meaning you don't have an estate tax problem and you don't need to buy an expensive solution to a problem that likely doesn't exist).

But to be fair, the next chart implies that one should consider the prudence that many advisors claim they take. So, let's use a static return of 7.35% (CAGR = 5.01%) with a standard deviation of 21.1%. This shows the identical performance (dividends included) of the S&P 500 from 1997 to 2009.

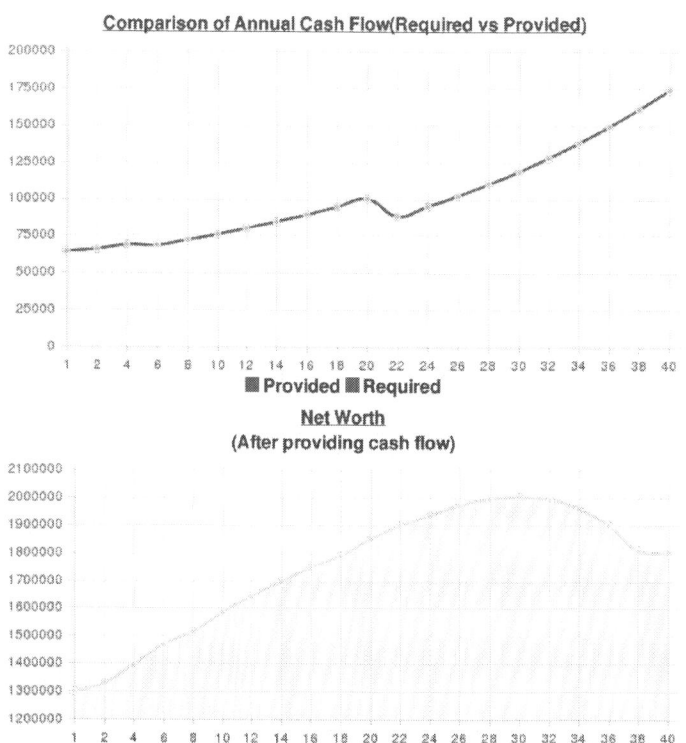

Now you have an ending net worth of $1.8 million. We have demonstrated prudence with conservative performance, and we have something that both the advisor and client can be happy with. That's more accurate and fair, right? Not exactly.

The first indicator that it's not accurate is the smooth acceleration and deceleration of net worth. Since when is anything smooth in the world of money?

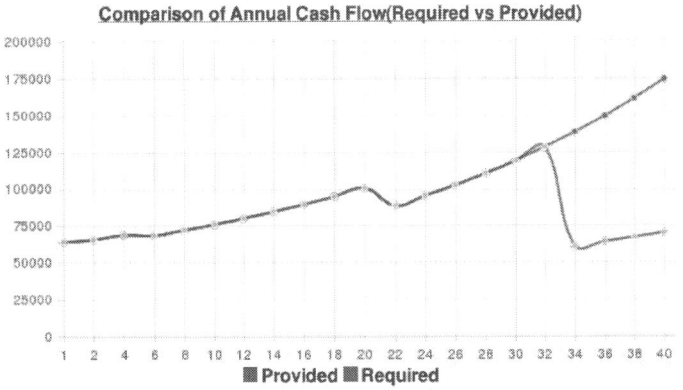

By comparing the previous chart to the application of market dynamics in the chart above, you can see that you now have a shortfall in year 33 of your plan and subsequently zero net worth. Twenty million to broke takes a lot of doing.

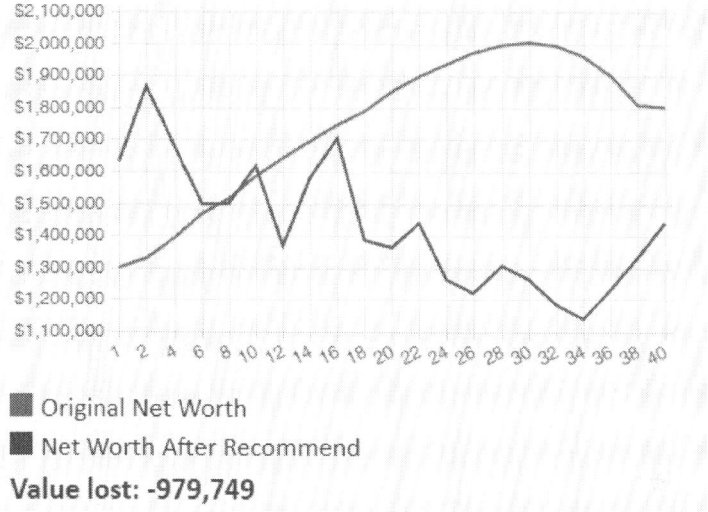

■ Original Net Worth
■ Net Worth After Recommend
Value lost: -979,749

What clients are being shown time and again is a beautiful slope that is psychologically easy to swallow, but the reality is the jagged blue line that (in this case) initially performs better because of the tear the market was on in the early years (1997–1999).

But as time rolls on, you can see the effects of volatility as opposed to the beautiful static and conservative returns, even though they are the *same* average. And the difference of almost $1 million (just comparing the last scenario) is enough to warrant additional work with holistic planning. Without this understanding, the advisor's work stops at a seemingly solid scenario ($20 million) that clients just like you are happy with – at first. Let's talk about another problematic issue.

Monte Carlo Simulators

LifeLock once ran a hilarious commercial. It opens with a bank robbery, where the assailants are yelling for everyone to get on the floor. A nervous lady looks up at the guy dressed in a guard's uniform and instructs him to do something, to which he replies, "I'm not a security guard. I'm a security monitor. I only notify people if there is a robbery."

Looking at the robbers and then back at her, he states, "There's a robbery."

The point of the commercial asks the same question that could be asked of advisors: "Why monitor a problem if you don't fix it?"

When an architect draws up plans for a building, they don't give a probability of whether the building will be built. No, the building is thought out down to the last detail and built by measuring twice and cutting once.

Sure, the owner may make changes to some aspects of the building, like the fit and finish, as the process unfolds, but that doesn't mean the building has a probability of not being built. So, why do advisors give clients a probability of whether they will plan their successful future? The advisor either will or won't.

Monte Carlo is fascinating to me, but there are two main reasons why I decided not to use it with my clients:

1. To achieve realistic output, hundreds of inputs need to be accounted for (which are not with Monte Carlo) relative to the client and the spouse, including (but not limited to):
    a. Investment distributions
    b. Various income needs
    c. Possible surplus or deficit in any given year
    d. One-time purchases
    e. Emergency needs
    f. Social Security options
    g. Guaranteed income benefit (GIB) variations
    h. Income tax
    i. Estate tax
    j. Capital gains tax
    k. Life expectancy
    l. Age of retirement

Essentially, what's available and commonly used as a tool is nowhere even close to cutting it, which makes a potential serious planning tool a novelty of sorts and places us squarely back in the position of having to plan anyway.

2. Monte Carlo makes selling the portfolio or investment the priority.

When you have a tool that assesses each portfolio to project the probability of outcomes, it's easy to get caught up in what I call "portfolio as a priority," a dangerous proposition I'll explain later. When the portfolio is the priority, planning takes a backseat, which is to say that planning is executed only to the extent that gaps are identified, therefore placing focus on the products needed to fill those holes. Advisors know this, and I have seen their behavior change dramatically when presenting to clients.

When advisors know that there are areas that haven't been given the needed thought, it becomes easier to talk over their clients, which I believe is due to their subconscious covering up the fact that they have offered very little value. It often comes out sounding like this:

Mr. and Mrs. Client, as you can see, I have prepared a Monte Carlo simulation, which is the same intense mathematical theory used in developing the hydrogen bomb. What we are doing is accounting for the "drift," which is the historical average of the periodic daily returns of your assets eroded by volatility at the rate of half the variance over time.

Time out... What!? It reminds me of a quote: "it takes a lot of words to cover up a lie." Look, it takes more work to take a period like 2000–2009 (the "lost decade") and use that as an acid test for which an advisor's time and knowledge should shore up all the shortcomings. This is why I say it encourages portfolio as priority. They want to sell you on investing in their portfolio, and it's far easier for them to speak over your head using a fancy tool that really has no teeth. Besides that, the Monte Carlo simulator:

- Cannot perform the analysis on all accounts for a holistic assessment.
- Cannot demonstrate deep losses.
- Cannot help plan for you outliving your money.
- Has a high propensity to use longer periods for a more accurate average, which actually throws the probabilities into unrealistic territory and gives you a false sense of security.

Why Advisors Don't Provide Quality Plans

"People pretend not to like grapes when the vines are too high for them to reach."

– Marguerite de Navarre, French author, 1492–1549

A 2013 survey revealed:

> An overwhelming majority of consumers (91%) expect the advice they receive from a financial advisor to consider their total financial situation. This expectation was largely consistent across all age groups. And, no other category of concern came close. I will note, however, that "something else" was placed as a category. In lieu of that, had "communication" been added as an attribute then this may have ranked close to, if not higher than, "strong knowledge of financial planning.[26]

---

[26] CFP Board. "CONSUMERS WANT ADVISERS TO FOCUS ON FINANCIAL PLANNING." Aug 20, 2013. https://www.cfp.net/news-events/latest-news/2013/08/20/consumers-want-advisers-to-focus-on-financial-planning.

WHAT ADVISOR ATTRIBUTES DO YOU PREFER?	AGE GROUPS				
	18-34	35-44	45-54	55-64	65+
Strong knowledge of financial planning	57%	47%	48%	43%	37%
Ethics	16%	15%	18%	19%	34%
Years of experience	17%	18%	18%	17%	13%
Large product offering	8%	17%	17%	15%	6%
Something else	2%	2%	3%	5%	10%

The report of the survey went on to say that more than three to one surveyed preferred their advisors to have knowledge in multiple financial areas, as opposed to specialized knowledge.

There are over 300,000 advisors in the United States, and according to FINRA, there are over 175 designations and certifications available for their higher education.[27] One of the most recognized is the CFP (certified financial planner) designation. According to the CFP board, they have granted this designation to 76,000 professionals in the United States. I would be willing to bet that they and the other 174 programs combined have issued well over the number of advisors that exist in the US.

So, advisors are seeking higher knowledge, and they are hanging the proof on their walls in a picture frame. Their clients see it, and if they don't, advisors are likely to point it out at some point in the beginning of the relationship. According to Cerulli, six out of ten advisors describe themselves as financial planners, yet only 30% truly offer planning services.[28]

---

[27] https://www.finra.org/investors/professional-designations.

[28] "59% of Advisors Perceive Themselves as Financial Planners, But Only 30% Truly Offer Planning Services," Cerulli Report Press Release, January 19, 2012; Cerulli Quantitative Update: Advisor Metrics 2011.

If so many advisors exist that have been trained in or have a certificate in multiple disciplines and are self-described as providing financial planning services, why is it that they don't provide quality plans? I would say it's two-fold:

1. Lack of proper tools to provide the plans
2. Lack of practice (business) efficiency, which constrains the time needed to construct a quality plan

Immediate gratification syndrome drives advisors to seek success in every misdirected behavior they display, but ironically, it's that same behavior that limits their success. If they're focused on adding value for you, they will realize the business inefficiencies that prevent them from being of value. Then they can better identify and address your issues. If an advisor focuses first on being a person of value, they will have far more success than if they placed success as a primary target. Engaging in the financial planning process is critical, not only for the clients they serve, but also for the sake of creating a thriving business for themselves.

What I am trying to say is that if advisors were better businessmen and women, they would have the time for you. Because they aren't, you smell it, and when they try to get you to sign paperwork to become their client, you say: "Let me think about it." I am sure you sincerely mean to think about it, but do you know how?

The planning process is a powerful tool for advisors combatting the excuse of "Let me think about it" because the planning process is precisely that – thinking about it. Wouldn't it be great if you knew how to think for yourself? You can, and it's far easier than you might imagine.

10

LEARN TO THINK FOR YOURSELF

"He's a real nowhere man, sitting in his nowhere land, making all his nowhere plans for nobody. Doesn't have a point of view, knows not where he's going to. Isn't he a bit like you and me? Nowhere man, please listen. You don't know what you're missing. Nowhere man, the world is at your command."

– The Beatles.

Learn to Think for Yourself

You know why you should learn to think for yourself? Because no one's discovered how to tax your thoughts. You see, when you think, there exists introspection into causality, and when you exercise introspection, you find direction. Purpose often accompanies direction, and when you find purpose, there's a longing to fulfill it.

Most people wake up, go to work, come home, pay the bills, and complain. They often don't know why they wake up every day. They're essentially surviving as wandering generalities. Thinking is the mechanism by which we wake up and see. It allows us to open our eyes to the possibility around us. Thinking enables us to live our lives as a meaningful purpose as opposed to a wandering generality.

I can't imagine anyone who would want to consciously make the decision to be pushed around by the whims of life, but so many of us are. This is true because, if you don't know what you don't know, you can't think intelligently about it.

They might think about their money and be moved to do something about it but find they are without the tools to do so, as they are not equipped to synthesize and, therefore, not equipped to act decisively.

I'd submit people simply aren't empowered to think about their finances. There's too much selling and not enough empowerment. And no, financial planning and planners are not the answer – at least, not how we know them today.

Let's Make Math Fun Again!

"Numbers inevitably will lead a person down the path of reason."

– Pythagoras

In school, one of the first things we learned was simple arithmetic: adding, subtracting, multiplication, and division. These were the building blocks on which we would eventually learn how to complete more complex calculations.

The challenge for most of us when we were young was that we didn't see the benefit this math would have for us as adults. I suppose that's why they say youth is wasted on the young. As adults, most of us still don't grasp just how important it is to have a command of this language.

The beauty of math is that it empowers us to solve a problem where some variables do not exist. But in all fairness, if you asked a math teacher to help you calculate the internal rate of return for an investment you made in a business a few years ago, the formula would look like this:

$$0 = \sum_{j=1}^{k} \frac{1-(1+IRR)^{-nj}}{IRR}(1+IRR)^n - \sum_{l<j} nl + CF0$$

[29]

I wouldn't want to deal with trying to learn and retain that formula, and it's understandable that most Americans don't, either. But we still need a way to be effective when it comes to arriving at decisions that could make or break our retirement.

---

[29] Where n = number of cash flows, CF = cash flow at period j. And IRR = internal rate of return.

No matter how complicated a math problem looks, you need to know that it is only a series of the four basic things we all learned:

- Adding
- Subtracting
- Multiplying
- Dividing

The same is true for your financial life. If you can learn the basics of calculating financial problems, then you can eventually learn to think critically when faced with any financial issue.

I understand that this is not for everyone, and you may want to lean on someone you regard as an expert, which is fine. The purpose of this is to help you to see that there is a way to figure all your financial problems and a resource for this. But *really*, it's not rocket science! And if you can get past the mental block of "math + me = bad experience," you will have fun. Besides, your financial future depends on this math. It's practical!

Let's make math fun again, the math that effectively answers the burning question: "How does this help in a practical way in my life?" And, to do this, my self-paced courses will show you how to use an HP 12c (financial calculator). Now, unless you are an engineer or a finance major, you may not know how to use one. Don't worry; even many financial advisors don't know how to use this calculator. When you do, you can calculate:

1. Standard deviation
2. Internal rate of return
3. Time value of money
4. Effective annual rate
5. Capital value

All these basic calculations will help you determine:

1. Mortgage payments
2. Lease payments
3. Amortization on loans
4. Future financial needs like retirement, etc.

Not to mention critical thinking when it comes to things like what's more beneficial for you, a 15- or 30-year mortgage. This is critical for your financial future and can easily make a difference of several hundreds of thousands of dollars.

In my self-paced "Breakthroughs" course, I teach you step by step how to use this calculator, and all these calculations combined have a simple one-page cheat sheet for future reference.

Your Retirement Destinations

Fewer than 7% of financial advisors use a consultative (financial planning) approach.[30] If you happen to be an advisor getting excited about the possibilities of separating yourself from the 93%, or if you, as a client, are proud that your advisor is one of those 7%, you should remember the February 2011 article from *The Network Journal* in which the Society of Actuaries analyzed 12 financial planning software programs and concluded that financial planning software doesn't adequately address retirement risks.

In other words, 7% of advisors subscribing to the consultative approach more than likely are delivering a substandard service. It is for this reason that I have spent years perfecting a category-iterative planning methodology and creating planning software capable of fully incorporating this methodology.

---

[30] 2007 survey from *Best Practices of Elite Advisors: Wealth Management Edge* interviewing 2,094 advisors.

I believe every client has their own "financial fingerprint." However, all too often, clients are met with solutions that are one size fits all, where managing investments is prioritized and, in most cases, the issues in the clients' control are not addressed. When they are, these solutions lack the integration analysis that is critical to this process.

An example of this would be someone who is prescribed eight different medications from three different doctors. Each medication has its own specific properties that address a target issue perfectly. However, when other medications are introduced, they have a potentially adverse effect on each other. The more medications that are introduced, the more complicated the end solution becomes, and the more acute the attention to detail must be.

Wouldn't it be nice if you could push a button and all the complex calculations of your future financial life were solved? Or what if you could control the return on your stocks? Would you exercise that newfound power? Of course you would!

As you may know, you can only manage investment outcome. But with the right tools and proper planning, you can control the outcome with the decisions you make year by year.

Retirement success is more complex than simple rate of return. Proper decisions made today safeguard your future in down economies, steer you through sideways markets, and ultimately affect your financial standing tomorrow. Careful consideration of financial decisions leading to retirement and distribution planning in retirement must be the priority.

However, traditional financial services place the focus on assets and how those assets can fund a new financial product, while the concern for the lives supported by that money is clearly more important because everyone has their own financial fingerprint.

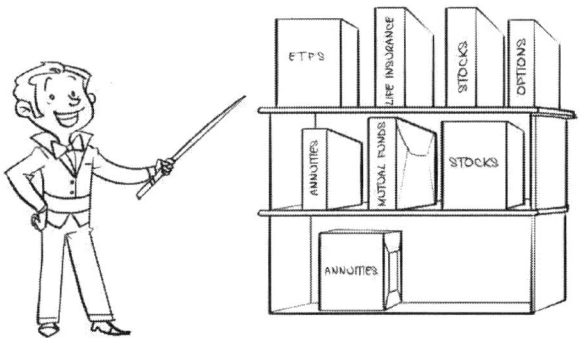

Tell me if this sounds familiar. Last time you sat with an advisor, the meeting probably went something like this:

"Currently your accounts are allocated like this, and according to historical data, this allocation should potentially return you 5% going forward."

"Having a balanced portfolio is like balancing your car tires. Left unchecked, it will cause unnecessary wear and potentially become fatal."

"According to your answers on our risk profile, your allocation should look like this."

"And according to historical data, you should expect 7% going forward if we reallocate, putting you closer to your retirement goals."

"But remember, past performance is no guarantee of future results!"

So, what's the challenge with this methodology? Well, there is no guarantee of the 7% return. Besides, the rate of return accounts for very little regarding a satisfying retirement.

You can't control the stock market, but you can control financial decisions that have a significant influence on retirement health. Therefore, it's important to subscribe to the idea of "control what you can, manage what you can't" by performing financial variance testing.

Financial variance testing, put simply, is asking multiple "what if" questions on over 50 critical areas of your finances, for example: How do we hold our debt? Should we buy an annuity? Does it make sense to convert to a Roth IRA? If so, how will we be affected?

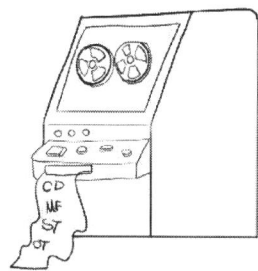

One of the 50 examples in my proprietary software algorithms is what I call "liquid asset priority." This calculates your specific scenario and determines the optimal order of asset liquidation during retirement to meet your funding requirements.

Liquid Asset Priority
1. CDs
2. Mutual Funds
3. Stocks
4. Variable Annuity
5. Fixed Annuity
6. Roth IRA

TAXES
RATE OF RETURN
FEES

Each account type, like CDs, mutual funds, stocks, etc., is separated by three major characteristics. These characteristics allow a gain or loss in efficiency, depending on the order you distribute assets, that has huge implications on your future financial stability. To illustrate, I have put together two scenarios, one reflecting the use of liquid asset priority and the other without.

Each scenario is identical in every way: the same account types, fees, returns, and beginning balances. Furthermore, each scenario reflects the same desired income, inflation rates for the same amount of years, and the same exact tax brackets. So, it makes sense that they would have the same financial outcomes, right?

CLIENT #1

For Mr. Sample, Age 65
& Mrs. Sample, Age 65

Liquid Assets (Taxable Interest)	$475,000
Liquid Assets (Tax Exempt Interest)	$175,000
Equity Assets	$200,000
Tax Deferred Assets	$350,000
Pension Assests for Mr. Sample	$150,000
Pension Assests for Mrs. Sample	$150,000
Total Liquid Assets	$1,500,000
Income Tax Rates	25.00%
C.D.'s	4.00%
Mutual Funds	8.00%
Roth IRA	8.00%
Muni Bonds	4.00%
Brokerage Account	
Growth Rate	5.00%
Dividend Rate	3.00%
Variable Annuity	8.00%
Fixed Annuity	5.00%
Pension Assets Mr. Sample	7.00%
Pension Assets Mrs. Sample	7.00%
After Tax Spendable Cash Flow Required	$60,000
Inflation Rate	3.60%

CLIENT #2

For Mr. Sample, Age 65
& Mrs. Sample, Age 65

Liquid Assets (Taxable Interest)	$475,000
Liquid Assets (Tax Exempt Interest)	$175,000
Equity Assets	$200,000
Tax Deferred Assets	$350,000
Pension Assests for Mr. Sample	$150,000
Pension Assests for Mrs. Sample	$150,000
Total Liquid Assets	$1,500,000
Income Tax Rates	25.00%
C.D.'s	4.00%
Mutual Funds	8.00%
Roth IRA	8.00%
Muni Bonds	4.00%
Brokerage Account	
Growth Rate	5.00%
Dividend Rate	3.00%
Variable Annuity	8.00%
Fixed Annuity	5.00%
Pension Assets Mr. Sample	7.00%
Pension Assets Mrs. Sample	7.00%
After Tax Spendable Cash Flow Required	$60,000
Inflation Rate	3.60%

There is a clear difference. The client who chose to not apply liquid asset priority runs out of money at age 89. Conversely, the client that does has earned an extra $764,000 by age 90 – in other words, a 50% return from the starting balance! That's a 2% return per year for 26 years! This was not from the performance of an investment but rather from making an educated decision!

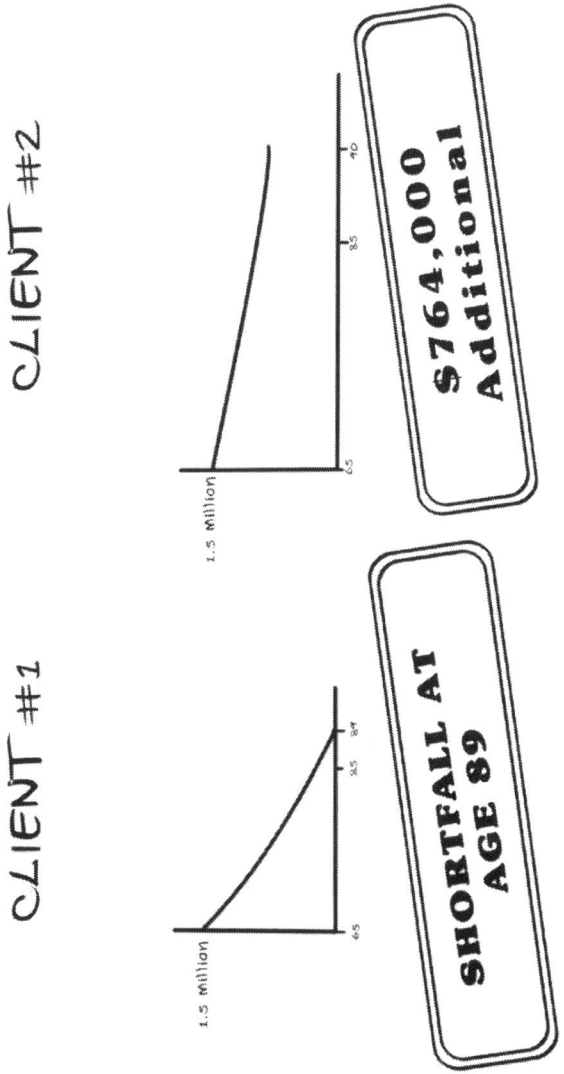

Client #2 can now enjoy retirement longer and possibly pass inheritance to loved ones. And by addressing over 50 other areas of financial variance testing, their retirement could be optimized even further. Controlling fees, taxes, and decisions that have positive outcomes equals a return on your money!

No one knows more about your money than you, and no one should care more about your money than you.

Noteworthy: It's better to live in the discomfort of your abilities than the comfort of your disabilities.

A great coach will groom you to think for yourself. Of course, if you truly want real and lasting financial change, you will have to be coachable.

11

ENSURING YOUR SUCCESS

"I can do things you cannot, you can do things I cannot; together we can do great things."

– Mother Teresa.

Tune in to Tap In

I have an old radio. It used to sit in my grandfather's woodshop and was always tuned to an AM station. I loved the smell of fresh-cut wood as I sawed and listened to talk radio in the background. Sometimes they'd play jazz or swing music from the 40s, which took me back to a different time. It was one of those experiences that make you love life.

To find your program you'd have to take a little time and effort to tune in to the signal just right so the words would come through loud and clear. It's one of the lost joys of listening to the radio, and like many of life's pleasures back then, before it could be enjoyed, we'd unwittingly have to apply a virtue of life.

Our success in life is much like an AM radio. You must tune in to receive the success signal, which starts by entertaining the right thoughts and saying the right things. This is critical because language is the software of the mind. Most find it difficult to think and talk positively, but I have found that the effort becomes infinitely easier when you think of others in the process. When we're thinking of only ourselves, our access to an exponential benefit from others is severely limited.

You must tune in to the right signal to tap into life's abundance. You have to tune in to tap in.

This IS the Ultimate "Pay It Forward" in Life

When you help others, you are not only potentially changing their lives in meaningful ways, but you are doing yourself a huge favor. Let me explain a little further, starting with reducing stress.

A 2015 survey by the American Psychological Association found that money is the leading cause of stress among Americans, and I have no doubt that this is also a global phenomenon. The interesting part is that this is not unique to working-class citizens.

Numerous studies on the effects of helping others have been conducted, and they all suggest that doing so reduces stress. We are all under a lot of pressure and often have bad days. At those times, it's difficult to think about anyone but ourselves, but too much focus on our own problems can lead to a downward spiral, one where the deeper we dive, the more we extract from others. But we are all on this merry-go-round together, meaning the people around you may very well be experiencing a bad day like you.

Keeping this idea at the top of your mind leads you to focus less on your problems and more on others, and the actions you take that result from this will ingratiate you with them. The simple offer of holding out a helping hand might be the very thing someone needs. After all, when we're in the dumps, it's common to feel that no one else cares.

Think about it. Each time you help someone, what is the response? Usually, it's a smile, a hug, or a fist bump. What does that do for you? Think back to the last time you helped someone. It made you feel good, right? And at that moment, you may have actually forgotten your own problems. Better yet, it may have put your problems into perspective.

When your problems are in perspective, there's a sense that they're not as overwhelming as you first felt. After all, isn't that what was causing your stress in the first place? The sense of being in an overwhelmed state of mind? The side benefit of this is that it gives you a sense of purpose and belonging. When you make it a point to help others, a sense of purpose unfolds. The people you help see you as a resource for good, and this sets in motion a personal sense of belonging.

Henry Thoreau said: "The mass of men lead quiet lives of desperation." Think about what that means. A self-serving life robs you and others of all you have to offer the world. There are wonderful things about you, like talents, experience, love and compassion, knowledge, certain skills, or energy, that can have powerful effects on those around you.

When you keep your blessings from other people, your life is bottled up, and you die with the music still inside you. Holding out on those around you serves to alienate you from a world that can embrace you as a positive force. Think about it. When we alienate ourselves from the world around us, our focus is on our job, our kids, our concerns. It's all about our life.

No wonder so many mothers become depressed when their kids grow up. No wonder so many men don't know what to do with themselves when they retire or lose their job. It's how they identified themselves and where they found their sense of belonging. But it doesn't have to be that way. Positive change is on the horizon. You don't have to be a wandering generality to others. You can be a meaningful purpose.

Becoming a "Meaningful Purpose"

Sharing the financial knowledge you have found can give you a sense of belonging. By doing this, you'll wake up each new day and live as a meaningful purpose, which combats depression. Empowering others with personal finance is what UGRU is all about. Helping others triggers the happiness trifecta. Science has shown that this trifecta consists of three different chemicals that have powerful effects on your mood.

When you help others, your body releases oxytocin, which counteracts cortisol (the stress hormone responsible for unwanted body fat). When oxytocin is present, so is serotonin, which is responsible for mood, digestion, sleep, memory, and your sex drive. And finally, helping others increases dopamine levels, which affects emotions, memory, and pleasure. When these chemicals are present, you can actually get hooked on helping others. And that's not a bad addiction to have.

The more you help others, the more positive your outlook on life is. Each time you help another, each time you witness elation or relief when a problem is solved, there is an amazing effect: it makes you feel like you've won a battle. You gain a sense that you've conquered an obstacle that someone else felt was difficult or, deep down, they may have lost hope of ever resolving.

Look, Mom may have said we are what we eat, but we are also who we hang around. And hanging out with negative people can easily have a negative impact on us. But if we understand the power we have inside of us to change another person's outlook, we are positioned differently. If we know the power of actively helping others, we become a meaningful purpose. And when we know our purpose has a positive outcome, the world change for us.

Our world now becomes filled with the possibility of positive change. This puts us in the company of positive people, who are elated and grateful that you helped them find money they didn't think they had, save money they didn't think they could, and have real and lasting financial change that gives them the same sense of self-empowerment that you received by helping them in the first place.

When you help people, you are on a "high," an oxytocin, serotonin, and dopamine high that makes you feel unstoppable. You feel like you can do anything. When you help others, you see that they are moved emotionally. They're moved because they're learning something powerful, and when they learn something powerful that resonates with them, it flips a switch inside called passion. Once that passion is turned on, it's nearly impossible to refrain from wanting to influence people with the same knowledge they've just learned.

When you see that unfold in front of your eyes, you have a sense that you're an agent of change for good. You see that you played an important role in someone's life being transformed for the better. You see the people you helped liberated financially because their finances are under control and they owe nobody anything, not even on their home.

You see that they love more and that they're more compassionate and charitable. You see their confidence spike, and life becomes fun for them! They see the world around them as possibility and want to help others achieve the same thing you have. It's contagious. And it's you that sparked it all. That is empowering!

Usually, when we start something in life, it's new and exciting. We revel at all there is to learn and are challenged to master that thing. As we master it, we go through a period where we're content to practice our art. But we live life knowing that there is nowhere to go from there, no higher level that we can achieve. And when we realize that the prize is only a t-shirt that reads "Been there, done that," we might be compelled to hold on to it because it reminds us that we are great at something, which means that the world needs us somehow.

Mastering something makes you ripe, and if you're ripe, you're rotting. If you're green, though, you're growing, and the questions become: What's left? What will give us that feeling we had years earlier when we first started that thing that made us look forward to the days ahead? Where is the fountain of youth? Where do we go to find youthful excitement that makes us eager for tomorrow as we fall asleep? And what will once again make us jump out of bed with purpose? How can we self-renew?

I would submit that self-renewal can only come from helping others. Helping others feeds your soul because you witness their lives transform. You experience the joy that comes with an epiphanic moment in their eyes, that point when you see they know their time has come, when they have that feeling of peace, that moment when they know everything is going to be ok. And that experience leads to a self-examined life.

Self-renewal happens when we self-examine and use that for the benefit of others. Plato said: "The unexamined life is not worth living." When we fail to examine our life, we become a wandering generality tossed by the whims of life, and the best we can claim is that we survived. But we weren't born to merely survive. We are here to thrive, to live life.

Andrew Klavan has an interesting twist on Plato's quote. He said: "The unexamined life is not worth living, but the unlived life is not worth examining."

Living can mean a lot of things: making enough income, pursuing a lifestyle, or simply breathing. But isn't living really when we feel most alive? When we feel less stress and more purpose? When we feel like we belong? When we feel happy, empowered, and continually renewed?

When you're in a constant state of helping others know what you know about money, it keeps you in a constant state of self-examination. And that self-examination keeps you making the right decisions with your own finances. Others aspire to emulate those decisions, which in turn feeds you the positive reinforcement needed to keep making the right financial decisions for yourself. In the end, it almost guarantees financial success and happiness.

Flawed Rational Perspective: Revisited

Early in the book, I presented a monologue from the Netflix series *Ozark* that offered some options for what money is.

Is it simply a*n agreed-upon unit of exchange for goods and services? Or is it an intangible? Security or happiness? Peace of mind?*

An intriguing third option was offered:

Money as a measuring device.

The following claim was made:

The hard reality is how much money we accumulate in life is not a function of who's president or the economy or bubbles bursting or bad breaks or bosses (which I agree with).

But then:

It's about the American work ethic. The one that made us the greatest country on Earth. It's about bucking the media's opinion as to what constitutes a good parent. Deciding to miss the ball game, the play, the concert because you've resolved to work and invest in your family's future. And taking responsibility for the consequences of those actions.

Patience. Frugality. Sacrifice. When you boil it down, what do those three things have in common? Those are choices.

Money is not peace of mind. Money's not happiness. Money is, at its essence, that measure of a man's choices.

That's a convincing argument, but if you watched the show, you know that the protagonist is making a case for why he behaves the way he does with money. He is justifying his shortcomings in life. Let me offer a fourth option.

Money is merely a measuring stick of the value that we lend to those around us. In other words, money is the byproduct of that value, and we have money to the extent that we lend value.

Noteworthy: *No one can enrich themselves unless they enrich others.*

Closing

I'll leave you with a few last contranyms. You can bolt from the responsibility of your finances, or you can bolt together a new financial future. You can model yourself after mediocrity or be a model for your children. You can be the person who left the masses, or you can be left behind. You can let the dust settle on your future or dust off your dreams. You can be bound for success or bound by your indecisions, cleave with your spouse for your future or be cleaved, buckle down or buckle under bad decisions, overlook your finances or be overlooked, pay rent or receive rent, strike out or strike now, move fast or stand fast.

What I'm trying to say is that you can be maligned or aligned. Position yourself to learn. Position yourself with a mentor and position yourself to help others, and you'll position yourself for a great financial future.

FINAL THOUGHTS

"She who succeeds in gaining mastery of the bicycle will gain the mastery of life."

– Susan B. Anthony

We can be taught how to turn the bars on a bicycle left or right, which will take us in new directions. We can be taught that pedaling forward moves us forward and pushing back on the pedals slows us down. But what cannot be taught is balance. For that, we must get on the bike.

Sure, we will fall, and sometimes it will hurt. But our falls will never hurt as bad as watching the other kids enjoy mastery of the bicycle.

Available from ugrucoaching.com discover:

- How you can enrich yourself by enriching others
- Self-paced personal finance courses
- Become a coach with certificates (coming soon!)
- How to think critically with the HP 12c
- How to think critically with financial planning tools
- One-on-one personal financial coaching
- Budgeting classes
- Budget tools plus much more!

ABOUT THE AUTHOR

Kenneth G. Gulliver

Ken was born in January of 1973. He attended the University of Phoenix and is a proud Marine Corps veteran. He has lived in three different countries but currently travels between Florida and North Carolina with his wife.

Free time is filled with church, exercise, boating, camping and community with friends. Each day he strives to be a better version of himself. Ken has an extensive background in financial services covering 25 years as:

- Public speaker
- Radio show host of Retirement Depot Radio
- Co-author of Asset Protection/Wealth Preservation
- Author of Right Where They Want You
- Author of The Unrivaled Advisor
- Co-founder of World Financial Group
- Top 1% Financial Advisor in USA (by revenue)
- Founder of Retirement Depot (a registered investment advisory firm)
- Founder/architect of UGRU Financial CRM (Cloud Awards finalist - CRM Solution of the Year)

Made in the USA
Middletown, DE
20 March 2020

86911059R10110